Aquinas on Mind

Topics in Medieval Philosophy
Edited by John Marenbon
Trinity College, Cambridge

In recent years philosophers in England and America have come to recognize the interest and importance of medieval philosophy. However, there are very few books to which the student and scholar can turn with ease. The choice is often between general studies which lack the rigour which philosophers expect, or specialist works which are hardly comprehensible to those not already deeply familiar with medieval ways of thought. This series provides books which consider problems and arguments in medieval philosophy in detail and with precision, but which do not assume any familiarity with the Middle Ages.

In the same series:

Modalities in Medieval Philosophy
Simo Knuuttila

Aquinas on Mind

Anthony Kenny

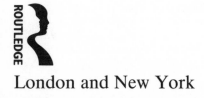

London and New York

First published 1993
by Routledge
11 New Fetter Lane, London EC4P 4EE

Simultaneously published in the USA and Canada
by Routledge
29 West 35th Street, New York, NY 10001

© 1993 Anthony Kenny

Typeset in 10/12 pt Times by Florencetype Limited, Kewstoke, Avon
Printed in Great Britain by Biddles Ltd, Guildford and King's Lynn

British Library Cataloguing in Publication Data
Kenny, Anthony
    Aquinas on Mind. – (Topics in Medieval Philosophy Series)
    I. Title II. Series
    189.4

Library of Congress Cataloging in Publication Data
Kenny, Anthony John Patrick.
    Aquinas on Mind / Anthony Kenny.
        p.   cm. – (Topics in medieval philosophy)
    Includes bibliographical references.
    1. Thomas, Aquinas, Saint, 1225?–1274.   2. Philosophy of mind
– History.   3. Mind and body – History.   I. Title. II. Series.
B765.T54K44   1993
128′.2′092–dc20   92–12224

ISBN 0–415–04415–4

Contents

Preface

My interest in the philosophy of mind of St Thomas Aquinas was first aroused in the 1950s by two professors at the Gregorian University in Rome, Fr Peter Hoenen, SJ and Fr Bernard Lonergan, SJ. To this day I regard Hoenen's *La Théorie du jugement selon S. Thomas d'Aquin* and Lonergan's *Verbum* as two of the most illuminating books about Aquinas' work in this area.

The relevance of Aquinas to contemporary philosophy of mind was later brought home to me by Professor Peter Geach and Father Herbert McCabe. Significant parts of the present book are the result of reflection on the texts of Aquinas undertaken in joint classes with McCabe in Oxford. I am greatly indebted to him and to the other scholars I have mentioned.

In 1989 I published a book entitled *The Metaphysics of Mind*. This was a systematic, not a historical, treatise, and its structure was based on that of Gilbert Ryle's *The Concept of Mind*. None the less, the philosophical account presented was influenced by the thought of Aquinas, and scholars will have been able to recognize many Thomist elements in the book.

For some years I have been collecting material for an explicit account of Aquinas' philosophy of mind. It is here presented not in a systematic structure, but rather in the form of a close reading of that part of St Thomas' *Summa Theologiae* which contains the most mature and comprehensive presentation of his philosophical psychology. The translations of the texts of Aquinas quoted in the course of my commentary are my own, but I am much indebted to the previous translations by Suttor, Durbin and McDermott mentioned in the Note on further reading.

I am indebted to Dr John Marenbon for the invitation to present this material in the Routledge series in medieval philosophy.

Oxford, February 1992

Abbreviations

In citing works of Aquinas the following abbreviations have been used:

A *In Aristotelis Librum de Anima*, ed. A. M. Pirotta (Rome, 1959), cited by lecture and paragraph number

C *In I ad Corinthios*, ed. R. Cai (Turin, 1953), cited by chapter and paragraph number

G *Summa Contra Gentiles* (Rome, Leonine Commission, 1934), cited by book and chapter number

H *In Libros Peri Hermeneias*, ed. R. M. Spiazzi (Turin, 1955), cited by book and paragraph number

M *In XII Libros Metaphysicorum*, ed. R. M. Spiazzi (Turin, 1950), cited by book, lecture and paragraph number

S *Summa Theologiae*, ed. P. Caramello (Rome, 1953), cited by number of part (1, 1–2, 2–2, or 3), question, article, and if applicable objection or reply; thus '1–2, 3, 2 *ad* 2' means: the reply to the second objection in the second article of the third question of the First Part of the Second Part

U *De Unitate Intellectus*, ed. L. W. Keeler (Rome, 1936), cited by paragraph number

V *Quaestiones Disputatae de Veritate*, ed. R. M. Spiazzi (Turin, 1953)

1 Why read Aquinas?

Why should anyone wish to study the philosophy or psychology of St Thomas Aquinas? He was an Italian friar of the thirteenth century, writing in low Latin encumbered with antiquated jargon, subservient to the teaching authority of the medieval church. Why should a secular English reader in the twentieth century expect to learn anything of philosophical value as a reward for the labour of working through the text of the *Summa Theologiae*? Surely, one may think, the progress of psychology in the centuries that have passed will have rendered obsolete everything Aquinas wrote about the nature of the mind.

The answer that one gives to questions such as these will depend, in the first place, on one's conception of the nature of philosophy. Philosophy is an unusual, indeed unique, discipline. Some people would claim that it was the most attractive of all disciplines, for the following reason. On the one hand, philosophy seems to resemble a science in that the philosopher, like the scientist, is in pursuit of truth. In philosophy, as in science, there are discoveries to be made. There are certain things which philosophers of the present day understand which even the greatest philosophers of earlier generations failed to understand. The philosopher, therefore, has the excitement of belonging to a continuing, cooperative, cumulative endeavour, in the way that a scientist does. Each practitioner may nourish the hope of adding a stone to the cairn: one may make one's tiny contribution to the building of the great edifice. And thus philosophy has some of the attractions of the natural sciences.

On the other hand, philosophy seems to have the attraction of the arts and of the humanistic disciplines, in the following way. Unlike works of science, classic works of philosophy do not date.

If we want to learn physics or chemistry, as opposed to their history, we do not nowadays read Newton or Faraday. Matters are different in the case of literature: when we read Homer and Shakespeare it is not merely in order to learn about the quaint things that passed through people's minds in those far off days. The same seems to be true of philosophy. We read Plato and Aristotle not simply in a spirit of antiquarian curiosity, but because we want to share their philosophical insights. Philosophy, then, seems uniquely attractive in that it combines being a discipline in pursuit of truth in which, as in science, discoveries are made, with being, like literature, a humane discipline in which great works do not become obsolete with age.

Medieval philosophy is obviously a fit topic for study by the historian, no less than medieval farming or medieval warfare. But if we are to justify the study of medieval philosophy by the philosopher, we need to form an opinion about the accuracy of the portrait of philosophy which I have just sketched. We need to decide to what extent it is true that there is progress in philosophy. Can we speak of a 'state of the art' in philosophy, as we can in scientific and technological disciplines?

Wittgenstein once wrote:

> You always hear people say that philosophy makes no progress and that the same philosophical problems which were already preoccupying the Greeks are still troubling us today. But people who say that do not understand the reason why it has to be so. The reason is that our language has remained the same and always introduces us to the same questions. As long as there is a verb 'be' which seems to work like 'eat' and 'drink'; as long as there are adjectives like 'identical' 'true' 'false' 'possible'; as long as people speak of the passage of time and the extent of space, and so on; as long as all this happens people will always run up against the same teasing difficulties and will stare at something which no explanation seems able to remove. I read 'philosophers are no nearer to the meaning of "reality" than Plato got . . .'. What an extraordinary thing! How remarkable that Plato could get so far! Or that we have not been able to get any further! Was it because Plato was *so* clever?[1]

Wittgenstein seems to imply a view of philosophy in which there is no real progress; or perhaps progress only in the sense in which there is progress in the expansion of *pi*. Since the days of

Pythagoras, mathematicians have made great progress in the expansion of *pi*; they can expand it to many, many more places than anyone could in ancient Greece. But in another sense, there is no progress; twentieth-century mathematicians are no nearer to the end of the expansion of *pi* than Pythagoras was. Is progress in philosophy like that, or is there genuine progress from age to age?

The answer depends on the relationship between philosophy and science and on the similarities and dissimilarities between the two. If you are a scientist and you want to do respectable work, you have to keep up to date: you must learn what discoveries have been made, what problems remain, and where current research is directed. You have to read the most recent periodical articles; in other words you have to know the state of the art. You need research equipment too which is up to the state of the art, the most efficient and expensive so far developed. The articles you write will quickly be dated: their shelf-life may be as little as five years.

Matters are of course quite different with the state of the real arts, that is to say, the fine arts. The painter does not have to look at what other contemporary painters are painting in order to paint well, and indeed it may be better for her painting if she does not. If she paints well, her paintings may remain objects of contemplation and admiration for years and centuries.

Some people think that in this respect philosophy resembles the sciences rather than the fine arts. If that is correct, then there is an obligation on the philosopher to keep abreast of current thinking and to be up to date in coverage of periodical literature. On this view, philosophy is a cumulative discipline in which recent work supersedes earlier work. We stand, no doubt, on the shoulders of other and greater men and women, but we do stand above them. We have superannuated Plato and Kant.

This view has recently gained wide favour among philosophers. It is perhaps more widespread in the US than in the UK, but on both sides of the Atlantic it finds most favour among those who work in the area of this book, namely philosophy of mind. Many philosophers of mind look forward to their work culminating in a fully fledged cognitive science. If this were a correct judgement of the nature of the discipline, then there would indeed be no more than an antiquarian interest in reading the works of medieval philosophers of mind.

In fact, philosophy is not a science, but it stands in a special relationship to the sciences. It has sometimes been described as the handmaid of the sciences, and sometimes as the queen of the sciences. I would prefer to describe it as the mother of the sciences. It is a commonplace that some disciplines which in earlier ages were part of philosophy have long since become independent sciences. The senior chair of physics at Oxford is still called the chair of natural philosophy. If we generalize from the history of philosophy, we can say that a discipline remains philosophical as long as its concepts are unclarified and its methods are controversial. Some may say that no scientific concepts are ever fully clarified, and that no scientific methods are ever totally uncontroversial. If that is true, all that follows is that there is always a philosophical element left in every science. But when problems can be unambiguously stated, where concepts are appropriately standardized, and where a consensus emerges for the methodology of solution, then we have an independent science rather than a branch of philosophy.

It is in that way that philosophy is the mother, or the womb, of sciences. It might, perhaps, be more appropriate to say that philosophy generates science not so much by parturition as by fission. What is meant by this can be illustrated by a single historical example: the question of innate ideas, which exercised philosophers considerably in the seventeenth century.

Initially the problem was set in these terms: which of our ideas are innate, and which are acquired? This broke up into two problems, one of which was psychological (what do we owe to heredity and what do we owe to environment?) and the other epistemological (how much of our knowledge is a priori and how much a posteriori?). The question of heredity vs environment was handed over, for better or worse, to experimental psychology; it is no longer a philosophical question. The question how much of our knowledge is a priori and how much a posteriori was a question not about the acquisition, but about the justification of knowledge, and that, after this first split, remained within philosophy.

But that problem, too, propagated by fission into a set of questions which were philosophical and a set of questions which were not philosophical. The philosophical notions of a priori and a posteriori ramified and refined into a number of questions, one of which was 'which propositions are analytic and which are synthetic?'. The notion of analyticity was in the end given a precise formulation, through the work of Frege and Russell, in terms of mathematical logic. The question 'Is arithmetic analytic?' was given a precise mathematical answer when Kurt Gödel proved his incompleteness theorem. But the mathematical anwer to the question left behind to philosophy many remaining residual questions about the nature and justification of mathematical truth.

In this case, then, we began with an initial confused philosophical question – the distinction between innate and acquired ideas. This then ramified in two directions – in the direction of empirical psychology on the one hand, and in the direction of precise mathematical logic on the other – leaving in the middle a philosophical residue which remains to be investigated and which will generate, no doubt, new non-philosophical questions in the fullness of time.

Does this mean that at some time there will be nothing left for philosophy to do? Will all problem areas be sufficiently clarified to set up as independent sciences? Anyone who looks through the collected works of Aristotle will find that the great majority of what he wrote belongs to disciplines which we would not any longer regard as philosophical. Aristotle's physics, his chemistry, his biology and so on are all now just a matter of the history of ideas, the prehistory of science. What remains worth philosophical study is his ethics, his philosophy of mind, his metaphysics and his epistemology. How long will they remain of philosophical value? Will all these disciplines finally hive off into new sciences?

I believe that the theory of meaning, epistemology, ethics and metaphysics will remain for ever philosophical. Whatever new non-philosophical problems will be generated by the study of these disciplines, to be solved by non-philosophical methods, there will always remain an irreducible core amenable only to philosophy. It is for this reason that the study of the philosophers of classical antiquity remains worthwhile, and that there seems to be no diminution in the interest shown by philosophers in the ethical and metaphysical texts of authors such as Plato and Aristotle.

In philosophy departments in the English-speaking world much more attention is paid to classical philosophy than to medieval philosophy. There are understandable historical reasons for this, and there are various ways in which the writings of Plato and Aristotle and Cicero are more accessible to the modern student than the writings of medieval schoolmen. None the less, there are a number of important ways in which a contemporary philosopher has more in common with his medieval predecessors than with his classical predecessors.

Most study of philosophy at the present time takes place in universities, and the university was a medieval invention, if by 'university' we mean a corporation of people engaged professionally, full-time, in the teaching of a corpus of knowledge, handing it on to their pupils, with an agreed syllabus, agreed methods of teaching and agreed professional standards. Philosophy was, in the Middle Ages, an extremely professional activity. The output of medieval philosophers was voluminous and systematic; and rigorous standards were imposed on philosophical discussion by the syllabus and the methods of instruction.

Many medieval philosophical and theological treatises bear the stamp of the academic disputation, which was one of the great instructional institutions of the Middle Ages. The teacher would put up some of his pupils – a senior student, plus one or more juniors – to dispute a philosophical issue. The senior pupil would have the duty to defend some particular thesis – for instance, that the world was not created in time; or, for that matter, that the world *was* created in time. This thesis would be attacked, and the opposite thesis would be presented, by the other pupils. In arguing the matter out with each other the students had to observe strict formal rules of logic. After each side had presented its case, the instructor would settle the dispute, trying to bring out what was true in what had been said by the one, and what was sound in the criticisms made by the others.

Voluminous output and rigorous presentation are two characteristics of medieval philosophers. A third medieval innovation is the syllabus. If there is a university syllabus then there are set topics, which any student is expected to master in the course of his studies. There is a corpus of knowledge that the student is expected to acquire before going on to make whatever original contribution he can to the ongoing scientific enterprise. There is a tradition which must be preserved, and then handed on to pupils, enhanced, one hopes, but certainly not diminished.

In the Middle Ages the syllabus was set especially by the surviving works of Aristotle. At the beginning of the high Middle Ages Aristotle's works were translated into Latin. Very few of the great medieval philosophers could read Greek, but they had good Latin translations; and they worked to assimilate all the knowledge that it was possible to extract from Aristotle and then develop it.

The academic philosophical community in medieval Christendom was more homogeneous than it is in contemporary

Europe. All universities used a common language, the Latin of the Church, and there was considerable migration of graduates between universities. Philosophical relationships between England and other European nations resembled those today between Britain and America rather than those between Britain and continental Europe. Divisions between academic communities in Europe began when the nationalistic wars at the end of the Middle Ages caused migration to diminish, and when the vernacular literatures began to develop. It is a significant fact that the last of the great medieval philosophers was John Wyclif, who is also well known for inspiring the first translation of the Bible into English.

The major difference between the philosophers of the Middle Ages and their classical predecessors or their modern successors was their universal acceptance of the inspiration of the Bible and of the teaching authority of the Church. But the effect of this should not be exaggerated. It did not mean that Scripture superseded the works of classical authors, or that theology rendered philosophy otiose. Christianity, it was believed, provided all the knowledge necessary for salvation: the humble washerwoman who knew the truths of the Christian faith and was completely ignorant of the science of the ancients had no less chance of getting to heaven and living in glory with God than someone as learned as Duns Scotus. But it would be quite wrong to think of the schoolmen as being interested only in religion. They were men of intellectual curiosity who wanted to know all they could about human beings and about the world. They were interested in human beings and the world as God's creatures, but they thought that much could be learned about the world not only through the sacred books, but also through the philosophical and scientific study of creation itself. When Aristotle was translated into Latin, in the twelfth and thirteenth centuries, scholars saw that beside the Christian tradition there was another corpus of information about the world, about human beings, about what kind of beings we are and what kinds of things we should do. This was to be found in the works of the ancients, and especially of Aristotle.

The history of medieval philosophy illustrates the point made earlier that philosophy propagates itself by fission. Within the medieval philosophical curriculum we find the germ of many of the sciences which set up as disciplines on their own after the Renaissance. In their infancy many sciences are to be found, as it were, as children growing up in the great household of philosophy.

The discipline of physics began as the study of natural philosophy, which was itself a programme set by the text of Aristotle called the *Physics*. Many of the sciences, such as botany, zoology or meteorology, trace their ancestry back to Aristotle and his school, and the most mature version of these sciences available to the early Middle Ages was still Aristotle's presentation of them. The Aristotelian works themselves traced out the philosophical syllabus for the medieval university.

The syllabus began with logic, itself a discipline created by Aristotle, which grew enormously in the Middle Ages. At the end of the medieval period scholars lost interest in the development of formal logic, and less attention was paid to the philosophical study of logic. It was only in the nineteenth century that formal logic was reborn, and the enormous renaissance in the subject led to the rediscovery, before and after the Second World War, of branches of logic which had been totally lost since the Middle Ages. In the last few decades scholars have come to realize that some of the most modern ideas of logic were things that were well known in the Middle Ages.

One way in which medieval philosophy stands closer to contemporary Anglo-American philosophy than post-Renaissance philosophy does is in the central role allocated to logic. Logic, in the broad sense, had a paramountcy in the Middle Ages which it has again today, but which it did not have in the intervening period. From Descartes onwards philosophers placed in the centre of their discipline not logic, but epistemology. Epistemology is the branch of philosophy which focuses on the question: how do we know what we know? How *can* we know what we know? The epistemological drive placed language and logic in the background. From the time of Frege and Russell up to the present day, at least in Britain and America, logic and language have once again been placed in the forefront of philosophy. The philosopher's great question in recent years has been not 'What do you know?' but 'What do you mean?' Philosophers have insisted that any question, whether in science or mathematics or anything else, must be accompanied by a very careful awareness of what we mean by asking it. This attitude is something that was very typical of the Middle Ages and is typical of philosophy once again at the present time.

If philosophy were a science, I said earlier, there would be no philosophical lessons to be learned from the study of medieval philosophy. But philosophy is not a science, even though it may give birth to sciences. The time has now come to examine a quite different view of philosophy, one which looks on philosophy as being exactly like a form of art. On this view, philosophy is essentially the work of genius, the product of outstanding individuals. If one sees philosophy as the succession of towering philosophical geniuses, then there is no sense in which Kant supersedes Plato, any more than Shakespeare supersedes Homer. On this view, philosophy can be engaged in as well by reading Parmenides as by reading Wittgenstein.

Like the opposite conception of philosophy as science, this view is an exaggeration which contains a kernel of truth. There is such a thing as progress in philosophy, whereas there is no sense in which literature progresses between one great writer and the next. But philosophical progress is largely progress in coming to terms with, in understanding and interpreting, the thoughts of the great philosophers of the past. It is true that we know some things and understand some things which the great philosophers of the past did not know or understand. But the things we know that they did not know are not philosophical matters. They are the scientific truths which have grown out of the sciences which have set up house independently of philosophy. With regard to the philosophical residue, the issues which remain philosophical, we are not necessarily in any better position than long dead thinkers. The reason for this is that philosophy itself is not a matter of knowledge, of acquiring new truths, but of understanding. And understanding is a matter of organizing what is known.

Philosophy is so all-embracing in its subject-matter, so wide in its field of operation, that the achievement of a systematic philosophical overview of human knowledge is something so difficult that only genius can do it. So vast is philosophy that only a wholly exceptional mind can see the consequences of even the simplest philosophical argument or conclusion. For all of us who are not geniuses, the only way to come to grips with philosophy is by reaching up to the mind of some great philosopher of the past.

This book is an attempt to reach up to the mind of one great philosopher, namely Aquinas, in one area of philosophy, namely the philosophy of mind. Throughout my own philosophical career, whether writing explicit history of philosophy, or first-order philosophy, I have been entirely dependent on the works of great past philosophers. There are four philosophers who, for largely

contingent reasons, have been the focus of my philosophical attention, namely Aristotle, Aquinas, Descartes and Wittgenstein.

These form a group of four contrasting thinkers. Aristotle and
Aquinas were systematic and scholastic philosophers, philosophers
who would come to mind as paradigms if one regarded philosophy
as a science. Descartes and Wittgenstein, on the other hand, fit
much better the more romantic view of philosophy as the single-
handed work of individual supreme geniuses. Aristotle and
Wittgenstein resemble each other in that both of them are fundamentally humanistic philosophers; though each of them pro-
nounced, from time to time, on issues of religion, most of their
argument proceeds without direct relevance to theology. Aquinas
and Descartes, on the other hand, were both philosophers to whom,
in different ways, the existence, omnipotence and omnipresence of
the Christian God were of fundamental systematic importance.

Aquinas, the subject of this present work, stands out from the
other three philosophers in various ways. He is much more accessible to non-philosophers than either Aristotle or Wittgenstein.
This may seem a surprising thing to say, since he wrote in a highly
technical Latin. However, once his technical vocabulary has been
mastered, his style is found to be simple and fluent. His syntax is
rarely ambiguous and the structure of each argument is laid out
with remarkable clarity. The ability to write philosophical prose
easily comprehensible to the lay reader is a gift which Aquinas
shares with Descartes, but which was denied to Wittgenstein and
Aristotle. Wittgenstein did, of course, write a plain and beautiful
German; the difficulty for the non-philosopher, reading his later
works, is not in construing particular sentences but in understanding the point of saying any of the things he said. With Aristotle it is
the other way round; it is clear that what he is saying is of immense
importance, but the problem is to discover what meaning it has, or
which of seven possible meanings is the intended one.

Aquinas stands out from all the other philosophers I have
mentioned in the sheer size of his output. Descartes's major works
can be read in two or three days, even though they repay rereading
over decades. Aristotle left almost exactly a million words, which
is about double the output of Plato. Wittgenstein published only a
very brief philosophical work in his lifetime; even when all that he
left unpublished has seen the light, it is unlikely to amount to more
than twice the *Nachlass* of Aristotle. In quantity of production,
Aquinas is quite beyond comparison. The works of St Thomas

were the first major corpus to be turned into machine-readable form for the purpose of constructing a computerized index and concordance. So we are in a position to say that in the less than fifty years of his life he produced 8,686,577 words. That is the total if one excludes all works where there is any possible doubt about authenticity. If the dubious works are included, the total reaches some eleven million. It seems probable that in one single, most productive, year Aquinas wrote about three million words. It is only since the computerized concordance was produced that it has been possible to have an accurate impression of the size of this output. Someone who has seen the word counts may well give credence to the evidence of witnesses at St Thomas' canonization that his method of working was to dictate simultaneously to several secretaries.

The enormous bulk of Thomas' writings has, indeed, been an obstacle to the serious study of his work. During the years when he was the official theologian of the Roman Catholic Church, seminarists were likely to study, instead of his own works, textbooks purporting to summarize his arguments and conclusions.

His greatest work, the *Summa Theologiae*, is itself more than a million and a half words long (half as long again as the surviving corpus of Aristotle). The major contemporary translation into English, the Blackfriars edition, occupies some sixty volumes. A serious study of the *Summa* could be a full-time occupation for a three-year university course. It is not surprising that Aquinas has been studied principally in epitome and anthology rather than read end to end. But it undoubtedly means that the sharpness of his thought has often been blunted in the presentation.

The other major obstacle to the study of Aquinas outside ecclesiastical institutions has been the belief that his philosophical integrity was compromised by his adhesion to the authority of the Church. If, in advance of any philosophical inquiry, he was committed to a detailed set of beliefs on fundamental issues, surely he was not engaged in any impartial inquiry, following the argument wherever it led, but simply looking for good reasons for what he already believed.

The first thing to be said in response to this allegation is that it is not necessarily a serious charge against a philosopher to say that he is looking for good reasons for what he already believes in. Descartes, for instance, sitting beside his fire wearing his dressing gown, was looking for good reasons for believing that that was what he was doing, and he took a remarkably long time to find them. Bertrand Russell was one of those who accused Aquinas of not being a real philosopher because he was looking for reasons for what he already believed. It is extraordinary that that accusation should be made by Russell, who in the book *Principia Mathematica* takes hundreds of pages to prove that two and two make four, which is something he had believed all his life.

One of the major tasks of a philosopher is to tell good arguments from bad, and the difference between good and bad arguments does not depend on the starting or ending point of the argument. Indeed, the distinction between what you believe and the reasons for which you believe it is something very relevant to Aquinas' philosophy, for he took great pains to bring it out in the distinction which he drew between natural and revealed theology. He was committed to many beliefs as a believing Christian, but there were many other things which he believed because he had read Aristotle and followed his arguments. He is careful to make a distinction betwen his beliefs as a theologian and his beliefs as a philosopher. As a theologian his task is to articulate, make explicit and defend the revelation about the history of the world, the salvation of the world and the future of the world contained in the sacred books of Christianity and the teaching of the Church. As a philosopher, his task is to get as far as he can in discovering what kind of place the world is, and what truths we can know which are necessary truths about the world and about ourselves, discoverable by unaided reason, without appealing to any alleged divine revelation.

One instance of his scrupulous adherence to these distinctions occurs in his treatment of the question of whether the universe had a beginning in time. There were a number of Christian philosophers who thought it could be proved that the world must have had a beginning; they thought this because they did not believe in the possibility of certain kinds of infinite series. Aquinas showed that their arguments were flawed, and urged that there was nothing self-contradictory in the idea that the world has gone on for ever and will go on for ever, as Aristotle believed. With unaided human reason, Aquinas believed, you could not prove that the world had a beginning. Equally, he believed, it could not be proved that it had no beginning, and here he takes issue with Aristotle, who thought it could. Aquinas as a philosopher is more agnostic than Aristotle: the matter is one which cannot be proved either way.

Why then did Aquinas believe, as he did, that the world had a beginning? In answer he would have appealed to the Book of Genesis: 'In the beginning God created heaven and earth.' That, however, was something he believed as a Christian theologian, not as a philosopher. It was not that he believed that one thing was true when you were doing theology and another thing was true when you were doing philosophy. There was only one set of truths: but some of them could be reached by philosophy alone, others only with the aid of divine revelation.

The contrast between philosophical and theological method comes out in the structure of Aquinas' two major works, the *Summa Contra Gentiles* and the *Summa Theologiae*. The *Summa Contra Gentiles* is meant as a philosophical work; it is directed to people who are not Christians, who may be Muslims or Jews or atheists. It aims to present them with reasons – reasons that any human being of goodwill can see to be good reasons – for believing that there is a God, that the soul is immortal and so on. The *Summa Theologiae* is very different in intent. It is addressed to Christians, and it accepts statements in the Bible as good starting points for arguments. But there is much pure philosophical reflection contained in that work too, even though its title describes it as a book of theology.

Probably the strongest reason for the neglect of Aquinas by professional philosophers has been the fact that he was accepted, both inside and outside the Church, as the official philosopher of Roman Catholicism. We have, in fact, just come to the end of the period in which that was true. Before the nineteenth century, though Aquinas was held in great respect, he was not in any way the Church's official philosopher. At most, he was perhaps the official philosopher of the Dominican Order. Then in the late nineteenth century Pope Leo XIII wrote an Encyclical Letter giving Aquinas a special place in the teaching of philosophy and theology in Catholic seminaries and universities. Since the Second Vatican Council Aquinas' influence on Catholic institutions has become much looser. His texts have been replaced by those of a variety of other and lesser philosophers. By contrast, the reputation of Aquinas in the non-Catholic world has gained from the fact that he is now no longer seen as the spokesman for a party line. In several parts of the world there is a growing interest in his work among people who are not Catholics, perhaps not Christians at all, but who are impressed by his massive philosophical genius.

2 Mind and metaphysics

Aquinas is well known among philosophers as a moralist, as a philosopher of religion and as a metaphysician, a theorist of being. If it is true that ethics and metaphysics are irreducibly philosophical, and if philosophy is a humane rather than a scientific discipline, then there may be good reason for studying what Aquinas has to say on these topics. But do his writings on philosophy of mind deserve attention? Is not this an area of philosophy which will shortly be, if it has not already been, superannuated by developments in cognitive psychology?

To answer this question, we have to ask what is meant by 'philosophy of mind'. And before answering that question in its turn, we have to address a more basic question. What is is meant by 'mind'?

Some people think of the mind as being a kind of inner environment, the polar opposite of the external environment of the physical universe. This, I shall argue, is not the correct way to think of the mind: the boundary between the mental and the material is not the same as the boundary between inner and outer. If we are to explore the geography of the mind, we must delineate the different mental faculties such as the intellect and the will; we must investigate the relations between the senses and the intellect; the contrast between outer senses and inner senses; the two kinds of imagination, fantastic and creative. The intellect is most helpfully thought of as the capacity for operation with signs, and the will as the capacity for the pursuit of rational goals. If we are to clarify what is meant by 'mind', we must also investigate the relation between the mind, the brain and the body. We have to trace the frontiers between our different cognitive capacities, and to relate the exercise of these capacities to their manifestations in our behaviour and their vehicles in our physical structure.

But why speak of the mind in these geographic terms at all? 'My mind to me a kingdom is', wrote the Elizabethan poet Sir Edward Dyer. Gerard Manley Hopkins also saw the mind as an inward territory, but for him it was a region of terror:

> O the mind, mind has mountains; cliffs of fall
> Frightful, sheer, no-man-fathomed. Hold them cheap
> May who ne'er hung there.

All of us, at one time or another, are inclined to think of the mind in similar, though less articulate, terms as an inner landscape, whether we look on it with delight like Dyer or with despair like Hopkins. Let us try to evaluate this metaphor philosophically. Let us ask whether, in prosaic truth, there is an inner region within each of us for us to explore; and if so, in what way philosophy can help us with the exploration.

It is not easy to give a non-controversial definition of the mind as a starting point for the evaluation of the metaphor of the inner kingdom. Different philosophers would delineate the boundaries of the kingdom in different ways. Historically, there was one conception of mind which dominated philosophical thinking in the centuries when Aristotle was accepted as the doyen of philosophers, and there has been a different one since Descartes inaugurated a philosophical revolution in the seventeenth century.

The old, or Aristotelian, kingdom of the mind had rather narrower boundaries than the new or Cartesian kingdom. For Aristotelians before Descartes the mind was essentially the faculty, or set of faculties, which set off human beings from other animals. Dumb animals and human beings shared certain abilities and activities: dogs, cows, pigs and men could all see and hear and feel; they all had in common the faculty or faculties of sense-perception. But only human beings could think abstract thoughts and take rational decisions: they were marked off from the other animals by the possession of intellect and will, and it was these two faculties which essentially constituted the mind. Intellectual activity was in a particular sense immaterial, whereas sense-perception was impossible without a material body.

For Descartes, and for many others after him, the boundary between mind and matter was set elsewhere. It was consciousness, not intelligence or rationality, that was the defining criterion of the mental. The mind, viewed from the Cartesian standpoint, is the realm of whatever is accessible to introspection. The kingdom of the mind, therefore, included not only human understanding and willing, but also human seeing, hearing, feeling, pain and pleasure. For every form of human sensation, according to Descartes, included an element that was spiritual rather than material, a phenomenal component which was no more than contingently connected with bodily causes, expressions and mechanisms.

Descartes would have agreed with his Aristotelian predecessors that the mind is what distinguishes human beings from other animals. But for the Aristotelians what made this true was that mind was restricted to intellect, and only humans had intellect; for Descartes what made it true was that though mind included sense-perception, only humans had genuine sense-perception. Descartes, that is to say, denied that animals had any genuine consciousness. The bodily machinery which accompanies sensation in human beings might occur also in animal bodies; but a phenomenon like pain, in an animal, was a purely mechanical event, unaccompanied by the sensation which is felt by humans in pain.

By introducing consciousness as the defining characteristic of mind, Descartes in effect substituted privacy for rationality as the mark of the mental. The intellectual capacities which distinguish language-using humans from dumb animals are not in themselves marked by any particular privacy. Whether Smith understands quantum physics, or is motivated by political ambition, is something which a third party may be better able to judge than Smith himself. In matters such as the understanding of scientific theory and the pursuit of long-term goals the subject's own sincere statement is not the last possible word.

On the other hand, if I want to know what sensations someone is having, then I have to give his utterances a special status. If I ask him what he seems to see or hear, or what he is imagining or saying to himself, what he says in reply cannot be mistaken. Of course it need not be true – he may be insincere, or misunderstand the words he is using – but it cannot be erroneous. Experiences of this kind have a certain property of indubitability, and it was this property which Descartes took as the essential feature of thought. Such experiences are private to their owner in the sense that while others can doubt them, he cannot.

Privacy of this kind is quite different from the rationality which pre-Cartesians took as the defining characteristic of mind. It is thus that human sensation falls, for Descartes, within the boundaries of the mental, whereas for the pre-Cartesian it fell without. When we come to look closely at Aquinas' account of the mind, we have therefore to realize that he not only describes it in a way different from Descartes, but has from the outset a different concept of the phenomenon to be described.

It is now clear that there is no non-contentious answer to the question 'Where are we to place the boundary of the mind?' The geography of the mind is not a simple matter to discover. Its most basic features are a matter of dispute between philosophers. It cannot be explored simply by looking within ourselves at an inward landscape laid out to view. What we see when we take this inner look will be partly determined by the philosophical viewpoint from which we look, or, we might say, by the conceptual spectacles we may be wearing.

I believe, as a matter of fact, that the clearest insight into the nature of the mind is to be obtained from the Aristotelian viewpoint. The mind is to be identified with the intellect, that is the capacity for acquiring linguistic and symbolic abilities. The will, too, is part of the mind, as the Aristotelian tradition maintained, but that is because intellect and will are two aspects of a single indivisible capacity. But whether or not this delineation of the mind is the most appropriate one for first-order philosophical inquiry it is, for obvious reasons, the one most helpful to adopt in a study of Aquinas' philosophy. Let us now therefore try to define more closely the aspect of Aquinas' philosophy to which we are to devote our attention.

Among philosophers in the Anglo-American tradition there has grown up, in the years since the Second World War, a branch of philosophy, a philosophical discipline, which is sometimes called philosophical psychology and sometimes philosophy of mind. The existence of the subject as a separate discipline in recent times was due primarily to the influence of Wittgenstein and secondarily to that of Ryle. In other philosophical traditions since the Renaissance it is not so easy to identify, as a specific area of philosophical study, the field which bears the name 'philosophy of mind'. This is because since the time of Descartes the philosophical study of the operation of the human mind has taken place in the context of epistemology. Epistemology, as I have said, is the discipline which is concerned above all with the justification of our cognition, the vindication of claims to knowledge, the quest for reliable methods of achieving truth. Epistemology, as contrasted with philosophy of mind, is a normative rather than a descriptive or analytic branch of philosophy.

Philosophy of mind is a particular pursuit of analytic philosophers. Naturally, the concerns which go under the name of philosophy of mind have not been absent from the syllabus of philosophy in the continental tradition. The description of mental states and processes and activities is, or should be, a necessary prerequisite for the evaluation, defence or criticism of them. But the special concerns and emphases of philosophy of mind have not been so clearly isolated from their epistemological settings in the continental tradition even in the works of those philosophers who explicitly set out to do so, such as Brentano and Husserl.

It was because of their radical anti-Cartesian stance that Wittgenstein and Ryle cleared the ground for analytical philosophy of mind. The anti-Cartesian stance was explicit, indeed blatant, in Ryle; it was tacit, but more profound, in Wittgenstein. The birth of analytical philosophy of mind was in fact a rebirth. For if we go back further than Descartes, to the Middle Ages, we find that philosophy of mind and epistemology are no less distinct in the medieval tradition than in the tradition stemming from Wittgenstein. Medieval philosophical disciplines, as was observed in the previous chapter, are distinguished primarily on the basis of the texts of Aristotle which lie behind them. In this way the *De Anima* is the medieval textbook of philosophy of mind just as the *Posterior Analytics* is the medieval text on epistemology, to the extent that the subject of epistemology can be clearly identified in advance of the Cartesian programme.

In the previous chapter I maintained that epistemology, ethics and metaphysics will remain for ever philosophical, and will never be superseded by non-philosophical disciplines. For this reason, I maintained, it was still rewarding to study ancient and medieval treatments of these topics. Is the same true of philosophy of mind? Many of my colleagues in philosophy departments would deny this. According to their view, the moment of parturition is now coming for philosophy of mind, and it is about to generate, perhaps already has given birth to, a new scientific discipline, cognitive science, which will leave behind it not a genuine academic discipline of philosophy of mind but rather a husk of superstition called folk psychology. If this is true, then it is indeed futile to turn to a medieval author for enlightenment on these topics. I believe the view stated to be completely mistaken; but rather than arguing directly against it I will try to refute it by showing, through a close reading of texts from Aquinas, that medieval thinkers do indeed still have much to teach us about the philosophy of mind.

Medieval philosophical disciplines, as has been said, were demarcated by the texts of Aristotle which set the terms of the syllabus. But of course since the greatest medieval philosophers were theologians first and philosophers second, it is to their theological treatises rather than to their commentaries on *De Anima* that one turns for their insights into philosophy of mind. The remaining chapters of this book will indeed take the form of a selective commentary on that part of the *Summa Theologiae* in which St Thomas gives an account of the human mind, from questions seventy-five to eighty-nine of the First Part. In the remainder of the present chapter I will set out some prolegomena to this commentary.

First, the reader who has no previous experience of reading Aquinas needs some explanation of the structure of the texts to be studied. In the last chapter, I explained that the technique of disputation was an important element in the medieval curriculum both for the education of the student and for the prosecution of research. The reader who opens the *Summa Theologiae* will discover that though, unlike some of Aquinas' other works, it is not a record of live disputations, it bears the stamp of the method of disputation on every page. Whenever Aquinas is going to present a particular doctrine or philosophical thesis, or theological thesis, he begins by presenting a number of the strongest arguments he can think of against the truth of his thesis. The method is a powerful intellectual discipline to prevent a philosopher from taking things for granted. It imposes on the researcher the question: 'Whom have I got to convince of what, and what are the strongest things that could be said on the other side?'

To illustrate the structure of the *Summa* I will quote one of its shortest articles. The *Summa* is divided into four major parts, each part consists of a number of chapters called 'questions', and each question is divided into a number of articles. Each article, slightly confusingly, is devoted to the solution of a single problem or question. What follows is a translation of the tenth article of question nineteen of the First Part, which sets out to answer the question 'Does God have free will (*liberum arbitrium*)?'

It seems that God does not have free will.

1 St Jerome says, in his homily on the Prodigal Son, 'God is the only one who is not, and cannot be, involved in sin; all other things, since they have free will, can turn either way.'

2 Moreover, free will is the power of reason and will by which good and evil are chosen. But God, as has been said, never wills evil. Therefore there is no free will in God.

But on the other hand, St Ambrose, in his book on Faith, says this: 'The Holy Spirit makes his gifts to individuals as he wills, in accordance with the choice of his free will, and not in observance of any necessity.'

I reply that it must be said that we have free will in regard to those things which we do not will by necessity or natural instinct. Our willing to be happy, for instance, is not a matter of free will but of natural instinct. For this reason, other animals, which are driven in certain directions by natural instinct, are not said to be directed by free will. Now God, as has been shown above, wills his own goodness of necessity, but other things not of necessity; hence, with regard to those things which he does not will of necessity, he enjoys free will.

To the first objection it must be said that St Jerome wants to exclude from God not free will altogether, but only the freedom which includes falling into sin.

To the second objection it must be said that since, as has been shown, moral evil is defined in terms of aversion from the divine goodness in respect of which God wills everything, it is clear that it is impossible for him to will moral evil. None the less, He has an option between opposites, in so far as he can will something to be or not to be, just as we, without sinning, can decide to sit down or not decide to sit down.

$$(S \ 1,19,10)^1$$

Every article in the *Summa* follows this pattern. First, reasons are given for taking the view which is opposed to that which Aquinas is going to defend. Sometimes, as in the first of the objections in this case, the reason will be an authoritative text which takes the contrary view. More commonly, as in the second of the objections here, it will be a philosophical argument which makes no appeal to authority but which is derived from an analysis of the concepts involved in the proposition which is up for question. The present article is unusual in presenting only two objections to the thesis to be defended: the usual number is three, and in some cases half a dozen may be offered.

Second, there follows the *sed contra*, a reason for taking the view which Aquinas thinks correct. In those works which are records of live disputations, the initial arguments are followed by a set of arguments of *prima facie* equal weight in the contrary sense; and it cannot be predicted on which side the judgement of Aquinas, as moderator, will fall. In the fossilized disputational schema of the *Summa* the *sed contra* almost always supports Aquinas' own thesis; and it does not consist of a set of arguments, but usually of some authoritative dictum which provides a peg for Aquinas' real reasons in the same way as a biblical quotation will provide a text for a preacher.

Third, there is the body of the article, introduced by the phrase *Respondeo dicendum*. Here, commonly, the main reasons for Aquinas' position are stated in detail. In most cases the body of the article is much more substantial than in the present sample, which was chosen precisely for its brevity.

Finally come the answers to the objections initially stated. Quite frequently the answers to objections offer a crucial clarification of issues which have remained ambiguous or undecided in the body of the article. Often, too, they go a long way to accommodate the opposite view which has been stated initially in the objections.

In the following chapters, I will summarize and interpret Aquinas' teaching without keeping close to the structure of each article of each question. But the reader will find the commentary easier to follow if the general pattern of Aquinas' argumentation is kept in mind.

Aquinas treats of the matters which interest us from questions seventy-five to eighty-nine. My commentary will not follow his text in the order in which he presents it, but will start some time after the beginning, and will treat of the early questions only at a late stage. This is because questions seventy-five to seventy-seven are densely packed with metaphysical technicalities, and provide a very difficult starting point for those unfamiliar with Aristotelian terminology. Moreover, the conceptual framework within which they operate is questionable in many respects, and it is unfair to Aquinas, and discouraging for the reader, if a commentator offers a series of negative criticisms of his philosophy of mind before presenting the positive insights which make it rewarding to study.

Undoubtedly, however, some of the metaphysical concepts presented in questions seventy-five to seventy-seven are indispensable for the understanding of the questions which follow. Accordingly, before going on to expound that section of the *Summa* which begins with question seventy-eight, I will make a brief and preliminary presentation of the relevant technicalities.

The first pair of concepts to be grasped are those of *actuality* and *potentiality*.

If we consider any substance, from a pint of cream to a policeman, we will find a number of things true of that substance at a given time, and a number of other things which, though not at that time true of it, can become true of it at some other time. Thus, the pint of liquid *is* cream, but it *can be* turned into butter; the policeman *is* fat, prone, and speaks only English, but if he wants to he *can* become slim, start mowing the lawn, and learn Latin grammar. Aristotelians called the things which a substance is, or is doing, its actualities; and the things which it can be, or can do, its potentialities. Thus the liquid is actually cream but potentially butter; the policeman is actually fat but potentially slim; he is potentially mowing the lawn but not actually mowing the lawn; he has the potentiality, but not the actuality, of knowing Latin. Very roughly, predicates which contain the word 'can', or a word with a modal suffix such as '-able' or '-ible', signify potentialities; predicates which do not contain these words signify actualities.

Actuality and potentiality are very general concepts. In Aristotelian metaphysics the contrast betwen the two is instantiated in a number of independent dichotomies. As instances of the contrast between actuality and potentiality we may consider the contrast between *accident* and *substance* and the contrast between *form* and *matter*.

The change from cream to butter is different from the changes which may occur in the policeman. In the one case, a parcel of stuff changes from being one kind of thing to being another kind of thing. In the other case, a substance, while remaining the kind of thing that it is, acquires new attributes. Change of the first kind is substantial change. 'Matter' is used as a technical term for that which has the capacity for substantial change.

In everyday life we are familiar with the idea that one and the same parcel of stuff may be first one kind of thing and then another kind of thing. A bottle containing a pint of cream may be found, after shaking, to contain not cream but butter. The stuff that comes out of the bottle is the same stuff as the stuff that went into the bottle: nothing has been added to it and nothing has been taken from it. But what comes out is different in kind from what goes in. It is from cases such as this that the Aristotelian notion of substantial change is derived. Substantial change takes place when a substance of one kind turns into a substance of another kind. The stuff which remains the same parcel of stuff throughout the change was called by the Aristotelians *matter*. The matter takes first one form and then another: first it is cream and then it is butter. When it is cream, the Aristotelians said, it has the substantial form of cream, and when it is butter, it has the substantial form of butter. A substantial form is what makes a bit of butter to be a substance of a particular kind. The word 'makes' here must not be misunderstood. It is used in the sense in which the 'heads' side of a penny is part of what makes the penny what it is, though it is obviously not some external force acting on it from without.

A thing may change without thereby ceasing to belong to the same natural kind: a man may grow, learn, blush and be vanquished without ceasing to be a man. Changes which do not involve change from one natural kind to another are called accidental changes. As in substantial change a substantial form is involved, so in accidental change an accidental form is involved. A man who catches jaundice loses an accidental form of pinkness and acquires an accidental form of yellowness. A man who learns Greek loses no accidental form, but acquires the accidental form *knowledge of Greek* where before there was no accidental form but merely lack (*privatio*) of the relevant form. In accidental change the subject of change – i.e. what changes – is not matter, but a substance of a particular kind: that is to say, matter informed by a particular substantial form.

When a substance undergoes an accidental change, there is always a form which it retains throughout the change, namely its substantial form. A man may be first P and then Q, but the predicate '. . . is human' is true of him throughout. What of substantial change? When a piece of matter is first A and then B, must there be some predicate in the category of substance, '. . . is C', which is true of the matter all the time? In many cases, no doubt, there is such a predicate; when copper and tin change into bronze the changing matter remains metal throughout. It does not seem necessary, however, that there should in all cases be such a predicate: it seems logically conceivable that there should be stuff which is first A and then B without there being any substantial predicate which is true of it all the time. At all events, Aristotle and Aquinas thought so; and they called stuff-which-is-first-one-thing-and-then-another-without-being-anything-all-the-time by the name 'prime matter' (*materia prima*).

The doctrine of matter and form is a philosophical account of certain concepts which we employ in our everyday description and manipulation of material substances. Even if we grant that the account is philosophically correct, it is still a question whether the concepts which it seeks to clarify have any part to play in a scientific explanation of the physics of the universe. It is notorious that what in the kitchen appears as a substantial change of macroscopic entities may in the laboratory appear as an accidental change of microscopic entities. The notion of matter and form concerns us in our present inquiry not in the context of kitchen physics, but because of the application of these concepts which Aquinas, like other medieval philosophers, made to the relationship between soul and body.

When scholastics said that changeable bodies were composed of prime matter and substantial form, they should not be taken to mean that matter and form were physical parts of bodies, elements out of which they were built or pieces to which they could be taken. Prime matter could not exist without form: it need not take any particular form, but it must take some form or other. The substantial and accidental forms of changeable bodies are all forms *of* particular bodies: it is inconceivable that there should be any such form which was not the form of such body. Moreover, according to strict Aristotelian theory, such forms were incapable of existing without the bodies of which they are the forms. Forms indeed do not themselves exist, or come to be, in the way in which substances exist and come to be. Forms, unlike bodies, are not made out of anything; and for a form of A-ness to exist is simply for there to be some substance which is A (*M* 7,1419–25).

According to Aquinas, however, there was one form capable of existing without the body of which it is the form, namely the human soul. Any human soul, on the Aristotelian account, is the substantial form of some human body. We must beware of thinking that when Aristotelians said that human beings were made up of matter and form, they had in mind the doctrine that a human being consists of a body and an immortal soul. That is not so: the human soul is related to the human body not as form to matter but as form to subject. That is to say, a human being *is* a human body;

the dead body of a human being, according to Aristotle, is not a human body any longer. Human beings, i.e. human bodies, like any other bodies, are composed of prime matter and substantial form; the substantial form of the human body, like the substantial form of any animal, is called a soul. The human soul differs from animal souls in being capable of separate existence and immortal.

It is indeed most commonly with regard to the life-cycle of living beings that Aquinas and his followers make use of the notion of prime matter and substantial form. Aquinas held that in a living creature there was only a single substantial form at a given time. Even though an animal can do many of the same things as a plant (for example, self-nourishment and propagation), this does not mean that it has one form in common with plants which makes it a living thing, and another form in addition which makes it an animal. It has a single specific form which enables it to perform all of its characteristic vital functions at every level. If I pull up a handful of celery from the vegetable patch and eat it all up, it is not true that there are some bits of water which were first part of the celery and are later parts of me: for there are no bits of matter which first had the form of celery and later had the form of humanity, *and throughout had the form of water*. The form of water is merely 'virtually contained' in the form of celery in the sense that whatever a bit of matter could do in virtue of being water it can also do in virtue of being part of an organic whole which has the form appropriate to celery.

It is not easy to know by what arguments, or even by the practice of what discipline, we are to settle the question how many substantial forms there are in, say, a living dog. Hence it is hard to know whether to agree or disagree with Aquinas that there is only a single substantial form in each substance. But it is correct to say that *if* a substance can have only one substantial form at a time, then the matter of which the substance is composed must be prime matter in the sense of being matter which at that time has no other substantial form.

Does that mean that matter is formless? In one sense, matter can, indeed, be said to be formless. For strictly speaking matter does not *have* forms. Its relation to form is not that of *having*. What has the form is the substance, the matter–form composite. Matter is a kind of potentiality: when air is turned into flame, this shows that the air had the potentiality of turning into flame. The matter which is common to air and flame is precisely their capacity to turn into each other. But the potentiality of being flame is not what has the form of air: it is the air that has the form of air, and the air that has the potentiality too.

Matter as characterized by dimension is for Aquinas the principle of individuation in material things. What this means is that, for instance, two peas, however alike they are, however many accidental forms they may have in common in addition to their substantial forms, are two peas and not one pea because they are two different parcels of matter. It seems that if we wish to avoid confusion in thinking about matter it is best to take it, not as potentiality, or as a part of a substance, but as a substance qua capable of change.

If we understand matter in this way, we can explain substantial form, correspondingly, as what makes a bit of matter to be a substance of a particular kind. When we say that form makes matter substance, we must again caution against misunderstanding: we are using the word 'makes' in the sense in which we might say that it is the Great Pyramid's shape which makes it a pyramid – we are not talking about one thing acting causally on another from outside, as when we say that rain makes the grass grow. Aquinas' favourite expression for a form is 'that by which, or in virtue of which, a thing is what it is' (*id quo aliquid est*). A substantial form is that in virtue of which a thing is the kind of thing it is: that, indeed, in virtue of which it exists at all. An accidental form is that in virtue of which something is F, where 'F' is some predicate in one of the categories of accidents.

The substantial forms of material objects are individual forms. Peter, Paul and John may share the same substantial form in the sense that they each have the substantial form of humanity; but if we are counting forms, the humanity of Peter, the humanity of Paul and the humanity of John add up to three forms, not one. What makes Peter, Paul and John three men and not a single man is their matter, and not their form; but the matter, in individuating the substances, also individuates their substantial forms. Aquinas would have regarded as unacceptable the Platonic notion that Peter, Paul and John are all men by sharing in a single common Form of Humanity.

True to his doctrine that if two things have similar substantial forms it is their matter which individuates them, Aquinas maintained that there could not be more than a single immaterial angel of any given kind. Peter and Paul belonged to the same species, being different parcels of matter with similar human forms; the archangels Michael and Gabriel were both unique members of a differing species, as different from each other as a human being is from a fish.

As I have said, Aquinas is prepared to allow an exception to his general thesis that the substantial forms of material objects exist only in the existence of the substances whose forms they are. The exception is allowed in the case of the souls of human beings.

There are serious philosophical difficulties in the identification of soul with form; or, to put the point in another way, it is not clear that the Aristotelian notion of 'form', even if coherent in itself, can be used to render intelligible the notion of 'soul' as used by Aquinas and other Christian philosophers.

One problem has already been mentioned. If we identify the human soul with the Aristotelian substantial form, it is natural to identify the human body with Aristotelian prime matter. But body and soul are not at all the same pair of items as matter and form. This is a point on which Aquinas himself insists: the human soul is related to the human body not as form to matter, but as form to subject (*S* 1–2,50,1). A human being is not something that has a body; it is a body, a living body of a particular kind. The dead body of a human being is not a human body any longer – or indeed any other kind of body, but rather, as it decomposes, an amalgam of many bodies. Human bodies, like any other material objects, are composed of matter and form; and it is the form of the human *body*, not the form of the matter of the human body, that is the human soul.

Another problem is this. Aquinas believed that the human soul was immortal and could survive the death of the body, to be reunited with it at a final resurrection. Hence, by identifying the soul with the human substantial form he was committed to believing that the form of a material object could continue to exist when that object had ceased to be. Consistently with his view that a human being was a particular type of body, he denied that a disembodied soul was a human being; but he insisted that it remained an identifiable individual, and this in turn led him into a series of inconsistencies. He had to insist that a human soul was individuated although there was no matter to individuate it, despite the fact that matter, on his own theory, is what individuates form. He maintained that individual disembodied souls continued to think and will after the demise of the human beings whose souls they are, in spite of his own frequent insistence that when there is human thought and volition it is not the intellect or the will, but the human being that does the thinking and willing (for example, *G* II,73). If the substantial form of Peter is what makes Peter a human being, how can it continue to exist when the human being Peter is dead and gone? A human being's being human is surely something that ceases when the human being ceases.

These difficulties will be evaluated in detail in a later chapter. In the present chapter, it is hoped, sufficient has been said about the main concepts of Aristotelian metaphysics to enable the reader to follow the presentation of Aquinas' theory of mind in succeeding chapters. Sufficient warning also, it is hoped, has been given of the problems which beset Aquinas' application of these concepts to put the reader on guard while following the lines of argumentation to be presented.

3 Perception and imagination

The senses are not, for Aquinas, part of the mind. None the less, the best place to begin the consideration of Aquinas' philosophy of mind is question seventy-eight of the First Part of the *Summa Theologiae*, in which Aquinas treats of the senses. This is partly because he himself describes the article as dealing with 'the pre-requisites of intellect' (*praeambula ad intellectum*), but also because when he goes on to treat of intellectual knowledge itself he will often explain what he has to say by making a contrast with his account of sense-perception. Moreover, when he talks of the five senses, even though he has comparatively little of philosophical importance to teach, it is immediately clear which faculties he is talking about. In the case of other cognitive powers, that is not always the case.

The senses are introduced as being one of the sets of powers which belong to the human soul. We will leave until later a consideration of whether it makes a difference whether a power, such as sight or hearing, is attributed to a soul or to a person; for the present we will proceed as if it is the same thing to say that something is a power of an animal's soul and to say that it is a power of a living animal.

Following Aristotle, Aquinas thinks that there are three different kinds of soul: the vegetative soul in plants, the sensitive soul in animals, and the rational soul in human beings. In a human being, there is only one soul, the rational soul, but it has a sensitive and vegetative part; these 'parts' are the set of powers which correspond to the sensitive soul in animals and the vegetative soul in plants (*S* 1,78,1,1 and *ad* 1).

According to Aristotle, there are, however, not just three but five different sets of powers to be attributed to the human soul:

vegetative powers, sensory powers, intellectual powers, appetitive powers, and locomotive powers (*De Anima* II, 414a29–32; *S* 1,78, *sed contra*). The lowest grade of powers are those which can affect only the body itself and its contents and products: these are the vegetative powers, namely the powers of digestion, growth and reproduction (*S* 1,78,2c). Other powers relate to objects outside the body, whether they are sensory powers with their restricted domain, or intellectual powers with a universal scope. The powers which relate to external objects operate in two directions: there are cognitive powers, which take in information (whether sensory or intellectual) about external objects; and there are those powers which are manifested in behaviour with regard to external objects (whether appetitive powers which set them up as goals to be pursued, or locomotive powers which enable the goals to be reached by bodily behaviour) (*S* 1,78,1c).

Different combinations of these powers produce different levels of living beings. Plants have only the vegetative powers, and can neither move nor feel. Immobile animals like shellfish can feel as well as digest, and they also have appetitive powers, because whatever can feel has drives, but they do not have locomotive powers since they cannot move from place to place (*S* 1,78 *ad* 3). Most animals in addition to the vegetative powers have the powers of sense and movement, and the appetitive powers that go with them. Humans, in addition to the powers of animals, have mind (which combines a cognitive power, the intellect, with an appetitive power, the will).

Since, according to Aquinas, whatever has a cognitive power automatically has a corresponding appetitive power as well, we may wonder why he wishes to count two different sets of powers here, rather than two different aspects of a single individual power in each case. We read in Ecclesiasticus 'The eye likes to look on grace and beauty, but better still on the green shoots in the cornfield' (40,22). Doesn't 'the eye' in this passage mean both the power of vision and the desire to see? Aquinas has an instructive reply:

> Every power has a natural tendency by which it desires its appropriate object. But animal appetite is something which is consequent on awareness of form. This kind of appetite needs a special power of the soul over and above the actual awareness. A thing is desired as it is in its own nature; but in a cognitive

power it is present not in its nature but by means of something else which is like it. Hence it is clear that sight desires a visible object only in order to exercise its own function of seeing, whereas an animal by animal appetite desires the seen object not only in order to see it, but for other purposes too.

(*S* 1,78,1 *ad* 3)[1]

Aquinas divides sensory powers into two categories: outer senses and inner senses. The outer senses are the senses properly so called, and Aquinas accepts the traditional list of five: sight, hearing, touch, taste and smell. Senses are to be individuated, he says, not according to diversity of organ, but diversity of function. A sense, he says, is a passive power whose function is to undergo change through the action of an external sense-object.[2] The outer source of internal change is the primary object of sense-perception, and it is by the diversity of these objects that sensory powers are distinguished. Thus, sight and hearing differ not because eyes are different from ears, but because colours are different from sounds.

Having said that a sense is a passive power to undergo change effected by an external stimulus, Aquinas immediately goes on to explain that a special notion of 'change' is here in play:

There are two sorts of change, one natural and the other spiritual. Natural change is when the form of the source of change is received in the changing object in its natural mode of being, as heat is acquired when something is heated. Spiritual change is when the form of the source of change is received in the object of change in a spiritual manner, as the form of colour is received in the eye without the eye thereby becoming coloured. The senses can only operate if there is a spiritual change whereby the intention of the sensible form comes to be in the sense-organ. Otherwise, if natural change sufficed for sensation, all natural bodies would feel whenever they underwent a change.

(*S* 1,78,3c)[3]

The last part of this is the clearest, so let us begin thence to decipher the passage. Feeling heat is something quite different from becoming hot; otherwise, whenever the sun shines on a stone and heats it up, the stone would feel the heat. So if we say that a sense is a power to undergo change, we have to say that it is a power to undergo a special kind of change, a spiritual change. The word 'spiritual' here is surprising. It is meant to make a contrast with natural, i.e. physical, changes; but Aquinas does not mean that anything ghostly or immaterial is happening. On the contrary he frequently emphasizes that the powers of the senses, unlike the powers of the mind, do not transcend the world of matter and can only operate under the appropriate physical conditions. In this context followers of Aquinas have preferred the word 'intentional' to the word 'spiritual', as being less misleading, and I shall follow them in this usage.

A sense, then, is the power to undergo an intentional change effected by an appropriate sense-object.

A sense is a power to *undergo*, not to initiate, change. Aquinas has in mind that the senses do not operate voluntarily: we cannot help seeing what is in plain view, or hearing the noise of the party next door, or tasting the nauseous medicine as it goes down, or smelling the rustic smells as we walk through the farmyard.

A sense is a power to undergo *intentional* change. The different senses, according to Aquinas, differ in the mode of their intentionality. Sight is the most purely intentional, he says; the intentional change takes place without any physical change in the organ or in the object sensed. In hearing and smell the objects sensed undergo change (the air has to vibrate for sound, and an object has to be heated to give off an odour). In taste and touch the organs undergo physical change: a hand is heated if it touches something hot, and the tongue is moistened in tasting.

The various accounts which Aquinas gives of the physical processes of sense-perception are almost always mistaken, and need not detain us. But it is worth spending time to get clearer about the nature of intentional change. The first thing to understand is that Aquinas' theory of intentionality is not intended to be an explanation of the nature of sensation: it is meant to be a philosophical truism to help us to understand, not to explain, what happens when an animal sees or hears. For explanation of the nature of sense-perception we have to look to the experimental psychologists, whose investigations have superannuated the naive and mistaken accounts which Aquinas gives of the physical processes involved.

Aquinas is surely correct to insist that the way to understand the nature of a sense is to start by looking at the objects which fall under it. Senses are essentially discriminatory powers, such as the power to tell hot from cold, wet from dry, black from white, loud from soft, high from low. Since there are many different ranges of qualities which we are able to discriminate, it will be to some extent arbitrary in which cases we say that we have more than one sense, and in which cases we say that a single sense can discriminate along more than one spectrum. Aquinas recognizes this, but he does his best to regiment our discriminatory powers so as to total the traditional number of five (*S* 1,78,3,3 and *ad* 3,4 and *ad* 4).

Some items which we can discriminate by means of our senses can be discriminated by one sense alone (for example, colour, sound); others can be discriminated by more than one: shape and size, for instance, can be felt as well as seen. The latter, which Aquinas calls the common sensibles, are all perceived by means of perceiving the former, which he calls the proper sensibles.

The way in which Aquinas' intentionality theory can cast philo-sophical light on the nature of perception is best understood if we contrast it with a different philosophical theory, the representational theory of perception. According to some philosophers, in sense-experience we do not directly observe objects or properties in the external world; the immediate objects of our experience are sense-data, private objects of which we have infallible knowledge, and from which we make more or less dubious inferences to the real nature of external objects and properties.

In Aquinas' theory there are no intermediaries like sense-data which come between perceiver and perceived. In sensation the sense-faculty does not come into contact with a likeness of the sense-object. Instead, it becomes itself like the sense-object, by taking on the sense-object's form; but it takes on the form not physically, but intentionally. This is summed up by Aquinas in a slogan which he takes over from Aristotle: the sense-faculty in operation is identical with the sense-object in action (*Sensus in actu est sensibile in actu*).

Let me illustrate what I take to be the meaning of this slogan with the example of taste. The sweetness of a piece of sugar, something which can be tasted, is a sensible object; my ability to taste is a sense-faculty; and the operation of the sense of taste upon the sensible object is the same thing as the action of the sensible object upon my sense. That is to say, the sugar's tasting sweet to me is one and the same event as my tasting the sweetness of the sugar. The sugar is actually sweet all the time, it always has a sweet taste; but until the sugar is put into the mouth its sweetness is not actually, but only potentially, tasting sweet.

Now a sensory faculty, such as that of taste, is nothing but the power to do such things as taste the sweetness of sweet objects. And the sensory property, sweetness, is nothing but the power to taste sweet to a suitable taster. Thus we can agree that the property in action is one and the same thing as the faculty in operation, though the power to taste and the power to be tasted are of course two very different things, the one in the sugar and the other in the animal. The sweetness of X just is the ability of X to taste sweet. (Of course it is related to various chemical properties and constituents of X; but that relation is a contingent one, to be discovered by empirical research.)

The theorem that the activity of a sensible property is identical with the activity of a sense-faculty seems to be something which is strictly true only of proper sensibles – qualities like taste and colour. It is only of these that we can say that their only actualization, the only exercise of their powers, is the actualization of sense-faculties. The common sensibles can actualize different sense-faculties, but they can also have quite other effects. A property such as heaviness can be actualized not only by causing a feeling of heaviness in a lifter, but in other ways such as by falling or by exerting pressure on inanimate objects.

Aquinas' theory of intentionality is not only, or mainly, a theory about sense-perception. In addition to maintaining the identity in actualization of sense-faculty and sense-object, he had a corresponding theorem about thought. Not only is the actualization of a sensible object the same thing as the actualization of the sense-faculty; so too the actualization of an object of thought is the same thing as the actualization of the capacity for thinking. *Intelligibile in actu est intellectus in actu*. This is an important topic to which we shall return in a later chapter.

In addition to the five senses, Aquinas believed that there were other cognitive powers which human beings shared with dumb animals. These he called interior senses, and he describes them in article four of question seventy-eight of the First Part. The interior senses are four in number: the *sensus communis* or unifying sense, the memory, the imagination, and a faculty which in animals is called the *vis aestimativa* and in humans the *vis cogitativa*.

Obviously, many animals share with humans the capacity for sense-perception; but as they also look for things which are not currently within the range of their perception, they also have some notion of what is absent. They can discriminate between, and derive pleasure or pain from, sensory properties; but this does not exhaust their discriminatory properties. If an animal is to survive, Aquinas says, he must seek and avoid certain things besides the things which are pleasant or unpleasant to the senses. If a sheep runs away from a wolf it is not because he dislikes the wolf's colour or shape; and a bird does not collect twigs for its nest because twigs feel pleasant to hold. The sheep flees the wolf because the wolf is dangerous, and the bird collects twigs because they are useful. Animals possess, therefore, some kind of awareness of danger and utility (*S* 1,78,4).

The power of grasping ideas which are not simply sensory ideas is called 'a power of estimation', *vis aestimativa*. Aquinas thought that such ideas were all inborn in animals, and so this power can not unfairly be called in English 'instinct'. Humans possess the same notions, but not by instinct; they acquire them by trial and error and association. In humans the ability to guess and verify what is dangerous and useful for the individual in this way is called the *vis cogitativa*. We are told also that the *cogitativa* is the faculty whereby he makes general judgements; it may be called the passive intellect or the particular reason (*S* 1,78,4; *Disputationes de Anima* 13). I know of no passage where St Thomas makes clear how the faculty thus defined is the same as the faculty introduced by reference to the notions of danger and utility.

The imagination is called *phantasia*: it is the capacity to produce *phantasms*. There are many passages in Aquinas where the word 'phantasm' would naturally be translated 'sense-appearance' or 'sense-impression' (for instance, *S* 1,74,6). But in other places it seems, as one would expect, that phantasms are produced by the imagination or fancy. The fancy is the locus of forms which have been received from the senses, just as, we will later be told, the receptive intellect is the locus of intellectual ideas (*S* 1,78,4). These forms or phantasms, we are informed, may be reshuffled at will to produce phantasms of anything we care to think about: we can combine, say, the form which represents Jerusalem and the form which represents fire to make the phantasm of Jerusalem burning (*V* 12,7). Clearly a phantasm is something like a mental image. But the two do not seem to be entirely equivalent.

Aquinas says that phantasms are particular in the way sense-impressions are. This does not seem to be altogether true of mental images. I cannot see a man who is no particular colour, but I may have a mental image of a man without having a mental image of a man of a particular colour, and I may imagine a man without being able to answer such questions as whether the man I am imagining is dark or fair. Again, we are told that there are phantasms which are produced by the *vis cogitativa*, whereas there could hardly be a mental image of *usefulness*; still, perhaps Aquinas in this context is thinking of the other definition which he gives of the *cogitativa*. But it also appears that he thinks that whenever we see something we have at the same time a phantasm of what we see; and he explains sensory illusions by saying that the senses themselves are not deceived, but only the *phantasia* on which they act (*M* 4,1,4). It seems odd to suggest that whenever we see a horse we have at the same time a mental image of a horse. Perhaps the theory is that if we see accurately our phantasm of a horse is a sense-impression; if we are mistaken about what we see, and there is no horse there at all, then our phantasm is a mental image. This theory seems to be confused in several ways, but it is hard to be sure whether Aquinas held it or not. At all events it seems clear that he did not mean by 'phantasm' simply a mental image.

In addition to an instinctive grasp of what is useful and dangerous, Aquinas attributes to animals a memory for such properties. He even attributes to them a concept of pastness as such, which many philosophers would find difficulty in attributing to a non-language-user. But he sees a difference between human memory and animal memory, in that while both humans and animals remember things, only humans can try to remember things or make efforts to call things to mind: in his terminology, animals have *memoria* but not *reminiscentia*.

Locke, like Aquinas, used the expression 'inner sense'. It was by this sense, he said, that men perceived the operations of their own minds. This corresponds to one of the functions of the *sensus communis* by which, Aquinas says, a man perceives himself perceiving. But faculties such as the *cogitativa* and the *phantasia* are first-order abilities to do things rather than abilities to observe oneself doing things. The two uses of the expression 'inner sense', therefore, do not altogether correspond.

It may be asked why a faculty such as the imagination should be called a *sense* at all. We can see some reason for it if we reflect that the power, say, to have visual imagery depends on the power to see. But St Thomas thought that this dependence was a contingent and not a logical matter (*V* 12,7), and in fact he places the connection between imagination and sense elsewhere. The inner senses, he thought, were like the outer senses in having bodily organs: only, the organs of the inner senses were inside the body and not at its surface. Thus, the organ of the *cogitativa* is 'the middle cell of the head', and the fancy has an organ which is injured in cases of seizure or coma (*G* 2,73). Now it is clear that the imagination has no organ in the sense in which sight has an organ; there is no part of the body which can be voluntarily moved in ways which affect the efficiency of the imagination as the eyes can be voluntarily moved in ways which affect the efficiency of sight. Moreover it is not possible to be mistaken about what one is imagining as it is possible to be mistaken about what one is seeing; a man's description of what he imagines enjoys a privileged status not shared by his description of what he sees. These are crucial differences between the imagination and genuine senses. Aquinas does indeed observe that others beside the perceiver may check up on what he claims to see with his senses, while in the case of the 'inner senses' there is no such thing as putting a man right about the contents of his mental image. But – as Aquinas does not seem to realize – this makes it inappropriate to speak of the imagination as a sense. For a sense-faculty which cannot go wrong is not a sense-faculty at all.

Aquinas' treatment of the inner senses is not one of the more satisfactory parts of his philosophy of mind. In my view, the whole notion of 'inner sense' is misleading; it is not the appropriate concept with which to grasp the nature of a faculty such as the imagination. The difficulty arises partly because Aquinas wishes to treat certain cognitive capacities of animals at the same time as he treats of the human imagination.

When we are talking of human beings there are at least two things which we can mean by 'imagination'. We may mean simply the ability to call up mental images: an ability which you can exercise now simply by shutting your eyes and imagining what I look like, or by sitting in silence and reciting the Lord's Prayer to yourself. Some behaviourist philosophers have denied the existence of this power, but obviously wrongly; it is a power which is very generally shared by members of the human race. What is more dubious is whether it makes sense to attribute mental images to animals, as Aquinas seems to do, since they do not exhibit the linguistic behaviour which provides the criteria by which we attribute the presence of mental images to each other.

There is another sense of the word in which imagination is a faculty much less evenly distributed among human beings. The ability to imagine the world different in significant ways; the ability to conjecture, hypothesize, invent – this is a second form of imagination, creative imagination. Creative imagination is what poets, storytellers and scientists of genius have *par excellence*. This is something which it would be more obviously absurd to call an 'inner sense'. If we are to distinguish between the senses and the intellect, this power is clearly an intellectual power. It is to the intellect that we now turn in following Aquinas as our guide to the geography of the mind.

4 The nature of the intellect

Aquinas' treatment of the mind in the *Summa Theologiae* begins properly with question seventy-nine, a long question with thirteen articles with the title 'On the intellectual powers'.

Before discussing the question, we need to say something about the translation of the crucial terms of the discussion. Aquinas' *intellectus* is fairly enough translated by the English word 'intellect': as we shall see, it is the capacity for understanding and thought, for the kind of thinking which differentiates humans from animals; the kind of thinking which finds expression especially in language, that is in the meaningful use of words and the assignment of truth-values to sentences. But English does not have a handy verb 'to intellege' to cover the various activities of the intellect, as the Latin has in *intelligere*. To correspond to the Latin verb one is sometimes obliged to resort to circumlocutions, rendering *actu intelligere*, for example, as 'exercise intellectual activity'. An alternative would be to use the English word 'understanding', in what is now a rather old-fashioned sense, to correspond to the name of the faculty, *intellectus*, and to use the verb 'understand' to correspond to the verb *intelligere*. In favour of this is the fact that the English word 'understand' can be used very widely to report, at one extreme, profound grasp of scientific theory ('only seven people have ever really understood special relativity') and, at the other, possession of fragments of gossip ('I understand there is to be a Cabinet reshuffle before autumn'). But 'understand' is, on balance, an unsatisfactory translation for *intelligere* because it always suggests something dispositional rather than episodic, an ability rather than the exercise of the ability; whereas *intelligere* covers both latent understanding and current conscious thought. When Aquinas has occasion to distinguish the two he often uses *actu intelligere* for the second: in such cases the expression is often better translated 'think' than 'understand'.

In the first article we are told that the intellect is a power of the soul. It is not identical with the soul; the soul has other powers too, such as the senses and the powers of nutrition (*ad* 3). But because the intellectual power is the most important of the powers of the soul, the intellectual soul itself is sometimes called the intellect.

What is the relationship between the intellect and the mind? Do we have here two words for the same thing? Following Augustine, Aquinas thinks of the mind as consisting not just of intellect, but of intellect plus will. The intellect is a power of apprehension, the will is a power of appetition; that is to say, understanding is an exercise of the intellect, love is an exercise of the will (2 and *ad* 2). Not all appetition is mental; there is also the animal appetition of hunger, thirst, lust; what is special about the will is that it is the power to want objects grasped by the understanding; it is a power of the mind: it is the power for intellectual appetition.

What is it that *has* the power which is the intellect? Aquinas is prepared to call it a power *of the soul*. This is because (as he has explained earlier, *S* 1,77,5) he regards thought as an activity which has no bodily organ. Because the activity does not involve the body, he goes on to say that the power, which is the source of the activity, must belong to the soul. But of course ultimately what the activity and the power belong to is the *person* who is performing the activity and whose soul and intellect are in question. Hence Aquinas says that in creatures the intellect is a power of the person thinking.[1]

If the intellect is a power, is it an active or passive power? Is it a power to act on something, or is it a power to suffer change? Aquinas' answer is that it is both. First he discusses the sense in which the intellect is a passive power. In thinking and coming to understand we undergo change:[2] that is to say, we start our lives in a purely potential state, with our intellect like a blank sheet with nothing written on it, and gradually we acquire understanding and our mind fills with thoughts. It would be possible to imagine beings who did not have to acquire the ability to think in the slow and toilsome way in which children have to be brought to the understanding of language. We might imagine creatures who were born with the ability to speak in the same way as we are born with the ability to hear. Aquinas believed that the heavenly angels provided an example of understanding which was exempt from the slow progress characteristic of human beings. They are throughout their existence in full possession of everything they will ever know. But human understanding is something very different, and so the human intellect is a passive power, a power to undergo change which needs to be acted upon by many factors if it is to realize its potentiality (*S* 1,79,2c).

The intellect considered as a passive power, the potentiality to receive thoughts of all kinds, is called by Aquinas, after Aristotle, the *intellectus possibilis* or receptive intellect (*S* 1,79,2 *ad* 2). It is contrasted with the *intellectus agens*, or agent intellect, which was described by Aristotle in the third book of his *De Anima* and which is discussed by Aquinas in the third article of question seventy-nine. If the function of the receptive intellect is as it were to provide room for thoughts, the function of the agent intellect is to provide furniture for that room, that is to create objects of thought. The material objects of the physical world are not, Aquinas believed, in themselves fit objects of thought; they are not, in his terminology, actually thinkable, *actu intelligibilia*. A Platonic Idea, something universal, intangible, unchanging and unique, might well be a suitable object of thought: but are there any such things as Platonic Ideas? To explain the function of the agent intellect, Aquinas gives the reader a brief lesson in ancient Greek philosophy.

According to Plato's theory, there was no need for an agent intellect to make things actually thinkable . . . . Plato thought that the forms of natural things existed apart without matter and were therefore thinkable: because what makes something actually thinkable is its being non-material. These he called *species* or Ideas. Corporeal matter, he thought, takes the forms it does by sharing in these, so that individuals by this sharing belong in their natural kinds and species; and it is by sharing in them that our intellect takes the forms it does of knowledge of the different kinds and species.

But Aristotle did not believe that the forms of natural things had an existence independent of matter; and forms which do exist in matter are not actually thinkable. It followed that the natures or forms of the visible and tangible objects we think of would not be, on their own, actually thinkable. But nothing passes from potentiality to actuality except by something already actual, as sense-perception is actuated by something which is already perceptible. So it was necessary to postulate a power belonging to the intellect, to create actually thinkable objects by abstracting ideas (*species*) from their material conditions. That is why we need to postulate an agent intellect.

(*S* 1,79,3)[3]

Plato's theory of Ideas, at least as Aquinas understood it, went like this. We see in the world around us many different dogs, each separate from the others, each living its own individual life. In addition to all these individual dogs, there is an Ideal Dog, which is identical with none of them, but to which they all owe their title to the name 'dog'. The Ideal Dog may also be called the Form of Dog; unlike individual dogs, it is not in space and time, it has no parts, and does not change, and it is not perceptible to the senses; it has no properties other than that of being a dog; it is The Dog, the whole Dog, and nothing but the Dog. Ordinary individual dogs, like Fido, Bounce and Stigger, owe to The Dog the fact that they too are dogs: it is by imitating the Ideal Dog, or sharing in the Form of Dog, that they are dogs.

What goes for dogs goes also for cats, and humans, and beds, and circles: in general, wherever several things are F, this will be because they participate in or imitate a single Form of F or Ideal F. By postulating these Forms or Ideas, Plato sought to explain, among other things, why many different things can all be called by the same name, and how the mind can have universal and unchanging knowledge about continually changing individuals.

In another passage (*S* 1,84,1) Aquinas explains how Plato was led to this position. The early Greek philosophers, he says, believed that the world contained only material things, constantly changing, about which no certainty was possible. What is in constant flux cannot be grasped with certainty, because it slips away before the mind can grasp it; as Heraclitus said, you cannot step into the same river water twice.

Plato, to save the fact that we can have certain intellectual knowledge of the truth, posited, in addition to ordinary bodily things, another class of things free of matter and change, which he called *species* or ideas. It was by participation in these that all particular tangible objects get called 'man' or 'horse' or whatever. Accordingly, Plato held that definitions, and scientific truths, and all other things pertaining to the operation of the intellect, are not about ordinary tangible bodies, but about

those immaterial things in another world. Thus the soul's thinking would not be about the material things around us, but about
their immaterial ideas.[4]

Aristotle and Aquinas maintained that there were no such things
as immaterial Ideas, and believed that Plato's method of accounting for universal knowledge led to absurdity. If the Ideas are
immaterial and unchanging, and all knowledge is of Ideas, then
there can be no knowledge of matter and change. That would rule
out natural science, and any form of explanation which involves
material or variable causes. It is ridiculous, Aquinas said, when
seeking information about things plain to view, to bring in strange
intermediaries of a totally different order. If there were any such
things as Ideas, knowledge of them would not help us in any way in
making judgements about the things we see around us (*S* 1,84,1c).

Aquinas and Aristotle were prepared to go along with Plato to
the extent that they would agree that what made Fido a dog was a
form – the form of dogginess or caninity, or what you will – but
they denied that there was any such form existing apart from
matter. Fido's dogginess exists in Fido, Bounce's dogginess exists
in Bounce, and Stigger's in Stigger. Fido, Bounce and Stigger are
all material objects in our familiar world, and in the real world the
only forms to be found are individualized forms like the dogginess
of Stigger. There is not, in the world, any dogginess which is not
the dogginess of some particular dog.

How, then, are we to account for the properties of our thinking
about dogs? We can think about dogs without thinking of any
particular dog; but there is no such thing as a dog which is no
particular dog. When we think a general thought about dogs, the
object of our thought is, we might say, the universal dog. It is the
universal dog which is the actually thinkable dog, the dog *actu
intelligibile*. But if Plato is wrong there is not, in heaven or earth,
any such thing as the universal dog. Plato's mistake is the attempt
to locate in the extra-mental world entities whose only home can
be in the mind.

Plato was misled because, believing that like can only be known
by like, he thought that the form of what is known is necessarily
in the knower exactly as it is in the known. He noted that the
form of an object of thought in the intellect is universal, immaterial, and invariant . . . . Thus he concluded that the things

thought of must exist independently in an immaterial and invariant manner. But this is unnecessary.

$$(S \ 1,84,1c)^5$$

How then do we explain the mind's capacity to have general
thoughts about dogs, when the only dogs there are to think about
are all individual? The answer given by Aristotle and Aquinas is
that the universal dog, the actually thinkable dog, is the creation of
the agent intellect. ' It was necessary to postulate a power belonging to the intellect, to create actually thinkable objects by abstracting ideas (*species*) from their material conditions. That is why we
need to postulate an agent intellect' (*S* 1,84,1c).

Here it is necessary to say something about the word *species*. In
the passages we have discussed it was first used as an expression
for Platonic Forms, synonymous with the Latin word 'Idea'. But
Aquinas goes on to use it in the exposition of his own theory.
'Intelligible species' are the acquired mental dispositions which are
expressed, manifested, in intellectual activity: the concepts which
are employed in the use of words, the beliefs which are expressed
by the use of sentences. My grasp of the meaning of the English
word 'rain' is one kind of species; my belief that red night skies
precede fine days is another kind of species.

The most natural English word to cover both concepts and
beliefs is 'idea', and in many contexts 'idea' makes an unproblem-
atic equivalent for 'species', and I will use it as such. If the English
word is dangerously ambiguous, that is all to the good, since the
Latin word is ambiguous in closely parallel ways.

Ideas may be ideas *of* or ideas *that*: the idea of gold, the idea
that the world is about to end. Similarly, species may correspond
either to the understanding of individual words, or to affirmation
and negation (*S* 1–2,55,1). Summarizing, we might say that ideas
comprise both concepts and beliefs.

Aquinas expounds the Aristotelian theory of the agent intellect
by means of a comparison between sense and intellect. Colours are
perceptible by the sense of sight; but in the dark, colours are only
potentially, not actually, perceptible. (In the daylight, they are
actually perceptible, but they are not necessarily actually perceived – perhaps no one is looking at them.) The sense of vision is
only actuated – the colours are only seen – when light is present to
render them actually perceptible (1,79,3 *ad* 2).

Similarly, according to Aquinas, substances in the physical

world are in themselves only potentially thinkable, because they are individual and thought is universal. To make potentially thinkable objects into actually thinkable objects, we need an intellectual analogue of light in the visible world. And it is this intellectual analogue of light which is the agent intellect. One can think of the agent intellect as like the lantern a miner carries in his helmet, casting the light of intelligibility upon the objects a human being encounters in his progress through the mysterious world.

What can we say about the agent intellect apart from this metaphorical description? First of all, it is an ability, or capacity, belonging to individual thinkers. For Aquinas, it is a natural endowment which each human being has; it is not – as it was for some other medieval Aristotelians – a supernatural agent acting on human beings from outside in some mysterious way (*S* 1,79,4).

The agent intellect is the power which humans, unlike other animals, have of acquiring abstract information from sense-experience. Animals with senses like ours perceive the same material objects as we do, but they lack the ability to talk about them, to think abstract thoughts about them, to acquire scientific knowledge about them. The species-specific ability which they lack is the agent intellect.

It helps to understand the kind of thing that Aquinas meant by 'agent intellect' if we consider human beings' ability to acquire language. Human beings are not born knowing any language; but it has been argued by the linguist Noam Chomsky that it is impossible to explain the rapidity with which children acquire the grammar of a language from the finite and fragmentary utterances of their parents unless we postulate a species-specific innate language-learning ability.

Even though Chomsky's innate language-learning capacity has to be an ability of a very general kind if it is to explain the learning of all the many diverse natural languages, it is not quite the same as Aquinas' agent intellect. While Chomsky, in talking about innate abilites, has in mind particularly the ability to master the internal structure of language, Aquinas is more interested in semantics than in syntax or grammar; he is concerned above all with the mind's capacity to understand meaning. Again the agent intellect, as we shall see, has functions which are broader than those of Chomsky's species-specific capacity.

None the less, for Aquinas the intellect is something very much akin to the ability to master language. For the intellect is a capacity, the capacity to think, and capacities are specified by their exercises: that is to say, in order to undertand what the capacity to *f* is, one must know what *f*-ing is. So to understand what the intellect is, we have to examine what its activities are; and according to Aquinas the various activities of the intellect may all be defined in terms of the use of language.

Following Aristotle, Aquinas maintained that intellectual operations could be divided into two types: the understanding of simple ideas (*intelligentia indivisibilium*) on the one hand, and affirmation and negation (*compositio et divisio*[6]) on the other. Both of these operations of the mind are defined by means of their expression in language. The understanding of simple ideas corresponds, roughly, to the mastery of individual words; affirmation and denial find utterance in affirmative and negative sentences.

Here is a typical passage where Aquinas makes his distinction between the two kinds of intellectual activity:

> There are, as Aristotle says in the *De Anima*, two kinds of activity of our intellect. One consists in forming simple essences, such as what a man is or what an animal is: in this activity, considered in itself, neither truth nor falsehood is to be found any more than in non-complex utterances. The other consists in putting together and taking apart, by affirming and denying: in this truth and falsehood are to be found, just as in the complex utterance which is its expression.
>
> $(V\ 14,1)^7$

The way in which the distinction between these two types of thought is linked with the difference between the use of individual words and the construction of sentences is brought out when Aquinas explains how any act of thought can be regarded as the production of an inner word or sentence:

> The 'word' of our intellect . . . is that which is the terminus of our intellectual operation: it is the thought itself, which is called an intellectual conception; which may be either a conception which can be expressed by a non-complex utterance, as when the intellect forms the essences of things, or a conception expressible by a complex utterance, as when the intellect makes affirmative or negative judgements (*componit et dividit*).
>
> $(V\ 4,2c)^8$

The two types of thought are distinguished by Aquinas with reference to the presence or lack of complexity. There are other types of complex thought beside the actual making of affirmative and negative judgements. Consider any proposition you like: let us take as examples 'Inflation leads to unemployment' or 'Angels have no bodies'. With respect to a proposition such as these, a judgement, affirmative or negative, may be made or withheld; if made, it may be made truly or falsely, with or without hesitation, on the basis of argument or on grounds of self-evidence. According to various combinations of these possibilities, the making or withholding of the judgement will be an instance of doubt, opinion, belief, knowledge or understanding.

Thus, one may refrain from making a judgement because of lack of evidence on either side, or because of the apparent equality of reasons pro and con. If one does make a judgement, it may be made on the basis of the alleged self-evidence of a proposition, or be the result of a more or less prolonged train of reasoning. Judgement may be tentative and hesitant, or firm and unquestioning. Aquinas classifies exercises of the intellectual powers on the basis of these different possibilities: the withholding of judgement is doubt (*dubitatio*); tentative assent, allowing for the possibility of error, is opinion (*opinio*); unquestioning assent to a truth on the basis of self-evidence is understanding (*intellectus*); giving a truth unquestioning assent on the basis of reasons is scientific knowledge (*scientia*); unquestioning assent where there are no compelling reasons for the truth of the proposition is belief or faith (*fides*, *credere*). Forming or holding a belief, accepting an opinion, coming to a conclusion, and seeing a self-evident truth are all instances of *compositio et divisio*; all have in common that they are intellectual acts or states expressible by the utterance of sentences.

There is, then, a very close relationship between thought and words, between the operation of the intellect and the use of language. But it is important not to overstate this relationship. Aquinas believed that any judgement which can be made can be expressed by a sentence (*V* 2,4). It does not follow from this, nor does Aquinas maintain, that every judgement which is made *is* put into words, either publicly or in the privacy of the imagination. Again, even though every thought is expressible in language, only a small minority of thoughts are *about* language. The capacity of the intellect is not exhausted when language has been acquired.

The understanding of simples is related to the entertaining of judgements as the use of individual words is related to the construction of sentences. An example of the understanding of simples would be the knowlege of what gold is – knowledge of the *quid est* of gold. Such knowledge can be exercised in judgements about gold, and without some such knowledge no judgement about gold would be possible. Some such judgements, such as 'gold is valuable' or 'gold is yellow', require no great understanding of the nature of gold; they presuppose little more than an awareness of what the word 'gold' means. A chemist, on the other hand, knows in a much richer way what gold is. Not only can she list many more of the properties of gold, but she can relate and present those properties in a systematic way, linking them, for instance, with gold's atomic number and its place in the periodic table of the elements. The chemist's account of gold would seem to approximate to the ideal described by St Thomas as knowledge of the quiddity or essence of a material substance (for example, *S* 1, 3,3 and 4,17,3).

However, Aquinas' account of the first operation of the intellect is not as easy to follow as his theory of judgement. The word (*verbum*) which results from the understanding of simples is not a judgement but a definition or *quidditas* (*V* 1,3c). Aquinas appears to use *quidditas* in two different ways and to give two correspondingly different accounts of the intellect's first operation.

In many places St Thomas observes that one can know what a word 'A' means without knowing the quiddity or essence of A. We know, for instance, what the word 'God' means, but we do not and cannot know God's essence (for example, *S* 1,2,2 *ad* 2). Learning the meaning of a word and acquiring a scientific mastery of the essence of a substance are both exercises of the intellect; but the grasp of essences is understanding *par excellence*. In the case of the understanding of simples no less than in compounding and dividing, we meet a distinction between a broad and a narrow sense of 'understand'. In the broad sense, the acquisition and application of any concept, the formation and expression of any belief count as exercises of the understanding; in the narrow sense, understanding is restricted to insight into essences and the intuition of self-evident truths.

Once language has been acquired, the thinker is in a position to use language to learn about the world – to think thoughts, make judgements, acquire knowledge and build up science about everything under the sun. This means, in Aquinas' terms, that the receptive intellect of an individual will be stocked with ideas about many things other than language. But what of the agent intellect? That is only one part of the intellect: is it a part which can be identified with the ability to master language? The identification here would be much less misleading; but here too there are qualifications to be made. For Aquinas the operation of the agent intellect is not the same as the acquisition of the mastery of a word: it is rather a prerequisite for it, the general ability to abstract ideas from the material conditions of the natural world. Chomsky, at least at one time, appeared to believe that there is a human language faculty which is distinct from the kind of general intelligence which a human, or an extra-terrestrial mind, might use in general computational activity. Aquinas' agent intellect, though like Chomsky's language faculty peculiar to the human species, would be involved no less in the acquisition of arithmetical concepts than in gaining mastery of syntax. Finally, as we shall see later, not every mastery of a word which a person would acquire in the course of learning a language like English would count, for Aquinas, as an instance of the abstractive activity characteristic of the agent intellect.

With these qualifications, however, it is helpful to think of the agent intellect as being in essence the species-specific power which enables human beings to acquire and use language in their transactions with the world which we perceive around us. As has been said, an animal with the same senses as ours perceives and deals with the same material objects as we do; but he cannot have intellectual thoughts about them, such as a scientific understanding of their nature, because he lacks the light cast by the agent intellect. On the other hand, for Aquinas, a being with an agent intellect but without the senses that we share with animals would be equally impotent to think even the most abstract and intellectual thoughts. In answer to an objection that if the agent and receptive intellect are both parts of the same soul, everyone will be able to understand everything whenever they want, he says this:

> If the agent intellect stood to the receptive intellect in the relationship in which an active object stands to a power, as a visible object does to the sense of sight, then it would indeed follow that we would immediately understand everything, since the agent intellect is what makes everything intelligible. But it is not itself the object of thought, but is rather that which makes actually thinkable objects; and for that we need not only the

presence of the agent intellect, but the presence of sense-experience (*phantasmata*), and sensory powers in good condition, and practice in operation; because understanding one thing leads to understanding others, and we pass from terms to propositions, and from premises to conclusions.

(*S* 1,79,4,3)[9]

The human mind has the ability not just to acquire concepts and beliefs, but to retain them. Aquinas, having introduced the agent intellect as the mind's concept-acquiring faculty, turns to consider memory, as the mind's capacity for retaining concepts and beliefs. He asks whether the memory is part of the intellect, and in reply he is led to make a number of distinctions.

Most of what we know comes only rarely before our minds. When I talk, whether aloud or in my head, I use only a tiny sample of my active vocabulary; when I listen or read, likewise, I draw on only a fraction of my passive vocabulary. We all know many facts, important or trivial, which we hardly ever call to mind or have brought back to our attention. We think of all these things as being somehow stored in our minds; and one of the things we mean by 'memory' is simply the ability to store ideas in this way. Memory in this sense, Aquinas says, is part of the intellect: it is identical with the receptive intellect, which, according to Aristotle, is the storehouse of ideas (*S* 1,79,6; 7 *sed* c).

Though the picture of the mind as a storehouse is a familiar one, we may well find it difficult to give an account of what is the literal reality which lies behind the picture. Avicenna denied that ideas could remain in the mind unthought of. We might speak without difficulty of things being stored in the brain; but how can things be stored in the mind? To be in the mind is simply to be an object of thought; so how can something still be in the mind when it is no longer being thought of? He concluded that when we reuse a concept, or recall a belief, we must go through the same process as when we first mastered the concept or acquired the belief.

Aquinas disagreed. There is an obvious difference bewwen learning something for the first time, which may take effort and calls for the appropriate environment, and making use of a skill already mastered, or bringing to mind a fact already known. Against the Aristotelians who agreed with Avicenna, he quoted the authority of Aristotle:

In *De Anima* III he says that when the receptive intellect

'becomes identical with each thing as a knower, it is said to be actualized; and this comes about when it is capable of acting on its own. But even then it is in potentiality, though not in the same way as before learning or discovering.' For the receptive intellect is said to become things when it receives the ideas of them. Having received the ideas of thinkable objects, it has the power to think of them at will, but it does not follow that it is always doing so. It is still in a manner in potentiality, though not as it was before first understanding; it is the kind of potentiality which a person has to bring to actual attention a piece of knowledge which is habitual.

$(S\ 1,79,6)^{10}$

In other places, Aquinas, followed by later scholastics, codified the different kinds of actuality and potentiality. A human baby, not yet having learned language, is in a state of remote potentiality with regard to the use of language: he has a capacity for language learning which animals lack, but he is not yet able to use language as an adult can. An adult who has learned English, even if he is not at this moment speaking English, is in a state of actuality in comparison with the child's potentiality: this was called 'first actuality' (S 1,79,10). But a state of first actuality is still itself a potentiality: the knowledge of English is the ability to speak English and understand it when spoken to. This first actuality can be called a *habitus* or disposition; it is something halfway between potentiality and full-blooded actuality (S 1,79,6 *ad* 3). The latter, the 'second actuality', is the actual speaking or understanding of English: particular activities and events which are exercises of the ability which is the first actuality (S 1,79,10).

Once I have learned English and still remember it, I am in this state of first actuality. Abiding intellectual abilities of this kind constitute one form of memory, and as Aquinas says, this kind of memory is not anything distinct from the power of the intellect itself. A power to acquire concepts and beliefs without the power to retain them would be something quite different from the human intellect; indeed, it is difficult to make sense of such a power, since a concept is itself an enduring understanding, and a belief is an abiding mental state, not a transitory mental episode.

But 'memory' does not mean only the retention of acquired knowledge. I remember the twelve-times table in the sense that I have learned it and not forgotten it. But when I say that I remember

being taken to the seaside at the age of 3, I do not mean simply
that I have learned, and not forgotten, that I was taken to the
seaside at the age of 3. The remembrance of a childhood visit to
the seaside is not, according to Aquinas, something which is purely
intellectual. Thus, he states the following argument against the
thesis that memory is part of the intellect:

> Memory is of past things. But the past is referred to by refer-
> ence to a definite time. Memory therefore is a way of knowing
> things in reference to a definite time, which is to say that it
> knows things by reference to here and now. But such knowl-
> edge is the province of the senses, not of intellect. So memory
> belongs not to the intellectual part of the soul, but to the same
> part as the senses.
>
> (*S* 1,79,6,2)[11]

Aquinas accepts the conclusion that if a memory is a memory of a
past object, considered as past, then it is not an operation of the
intellect, which is concerned with what is universal and timeless,
but an operation of that part of the soul, like sense-perception,
which is concerned with what is particular and temporal.

> Pastness can be considered in relation to the object known, or
> to the knowing itself. These two things go together in the case
> of sense-perception, which is acquaintance with an object
> through a modification brought about by a sensory quality
> which is present. Hence by one and the same act an animal
> remembers a past sensing of something and a sensing of some-
> thing past. It is not the same with the intellectual part: pastness
> is irrelevant to something when it is considered as an object of
> thought.[12]

This is because an idea such as the idea of *dog* is something which
abstracts from particular times and places, but is concerned only
with what makes a dog a dog. The word 'dog' applies equally well
to all dogs, past, present or future. The object we know when we
have mastered the word 'dog' is something to which any particular
time is irrelevant. But if we distinguish, as Aquinas does, between
the object known and the knowing itself, then matters are different. Any actual case of thinking about a dog will be a thought
thought by a particular individual at a particular time.

Our intellect's thinking is a particular act, occurring at one or other particular time, so that a man is said to think now or yesterday or tomorrow. This does not conflict with the nature of intellect . . . just as the intellect thinks about itself, even though it is itself a particular individual, so it thinks of its own thinking, which is an individual act which is either past present or future.[13]

This means, Aquinas says, that despite what he said earlier, there is in the intellect a kind of knowledge of what is past, as past: namely the knowledge which the intellect has of its own past acts. This seems surprising. Surely my memory that when I was 7 I learned Pythagoras' theorem is just as individual and particular a memory as my memory that when I was 3 I had a bucket and spade. So why does Aquinas want to make a distinction between the two? In fact, I do not think Aquinas is referring to memories of particular intellectual exploits in the past. What he has in mind is something different, along the following lines. If I know that whales are mammals, and call this knowledge to mind, then in the very act of such recall I know that this is something I have already known previously. (If I were in any doubt about this, my thought that whales are mammals would not really be a case of knowledge.) It is the awareness that one's knowledge of language, or of universal truths, is not something novel but something habitual that constitutes the element of pastness in intellectual memory.

Having discussed the relationship between intellect and memory, Aquinas goes on in the eighth and ninth articles of question seventy-nine to discuss the relationship between intellect and reason. Reason seems to be a peculiarly human faculty, since man is standardly defined as a rational animal. Is it the same faculty as the intellect, or something different (*S* 1,79,8,3 and *ad* 3)?

Aquinas' answer is simple:

> Reason and intellect cannot be different powers in human beings. This is clearly seen if one considers the activities of both. Understanding is an immediate grasp of an intellectual truth. Reasoning is passing from the understanding of one thing to the understanding of another thing in order to reach knowledge of intellectual truth . . . . So reasoning is to understanding as motion is to rest, or getting to having.[14]

The simplicity is a little deceptive: Aquinas has suddenly changed the focus of the noun 'intellect' and of the corresponding Latin verb *intelligere*, here translated 'understand'. Hitherto he has been talking of the intellect in the very general sense of the capacity for thought, and the verb *intelligere* has corresponded to the verb 'think'. Now he moves to a narrow sense of *intelligere* which means to grasp self-evident truths, and talks of the intellect as the power of such immediate understanding rather than of thought in general.[15] 'Human reasoning', he says, 'when engaged in inquiry or discovery, starts from truths immediately understood, namely first principles'. Reasoning and understanding, therefore, are two stages of a single process, and hence are activities of one and the same faculty.

Aquinas' text here can mislead in two ways, one trivial and one important. The switch of sense just mentioned, once it is pointed out, does not affect the argument. For understanding in the narrow sense of the grasp of self-evident principles is indeed an activity of the intellect in the broad sense. The power to grasp these principles is indeed, for Aquinas, the fundamental endowment of the intellect; that is why it is called *intellectus* in the strictest sense. The process of inferring conclusions from premises, which is the kind of reasoning which Aquinas here has in mind, is likewise a crucially important activity of the intellect. Aquinas is quite right to say that these are two parts of a single ability, two exercises of the same faculty.

What is seriously misleading is the suggestion that human intellectual knowledge can be laid out in an axiomatic system with self-evident propositions as axioms and the whole of science as a set of theorems from these axioms. Aquinas seems to have believed that every truth which is capable of being strictly known is a conclusion which can be reached by syllogistic reasoning from self-evident premises. There are some propositions which have only to be understood in order to command assent; such are the law of non-contradiction and other similar primary principles: the grasp of these is called *habitus principiorum*. There are other propositions which are proved from these by deduction; the grasp of those is called *habitus scientiae* (*S* 1,79,9c).

Aquinas nowhere gives a list of the self-evident principles which are the premises of all scientific knowledge, nor does he try, like Spinoza, to exhibit his own philosophical theses as conclusions from self-evident axioms. But he tells us that the findings of any scientific discipline constitute an ordered set of theorems in a deductive system whose axioms are either theorems of a higher science or the self-evident principles themselves. Thus, for instance, a conclusion of the science of optics may be derived from an axiom of optics which is itself a theorem of geometry (*S* 1,79,9c).

In the ancient world and in the Middle Ages Euclidean geometry appeared to be the paradigm of ordered knowledge, a paradigm to which, in due course, all scientific disciplines could be made to conform. We now know that even Euclidean geometry does not rest on self-evident axioms. But much more importantly, the axiomatic model of science quite misrepresents the relationship of scientific conclusions to the reasons for believing them to be true. The relation between even the best-established hypothesis and the evidence which confirms it is quite different from that between theorem and axiom in a formal abstract system. And even in the a priori sciences of logic and mathematics, Aquinas exaggerates the part played by syllogistic reasoning; syllogistic is only a small part of the predicate calculus, and there are areas, such as the logic of relations, which are beyond the reach of the medieval theory of syllogism.

Elsewhere in Aquinas we shall encounter elements which show that this model – derived from Aristotle's *Posterior Analytics* – is not the only one which he uses to represent the operation of scientific inquiry. But it is well for the reader of the *Summa* to be put on guard, at an early stage, against the damaging effect which this inappropriate model can have on Aquinas' exploration of the faculties of the mind.

5   Appetite and will

In question seventy-nine Aquinas discussed the intellectual powers of the soul in a general way. From question eighty-four onwards he develops his theory of intellect in a series of detailed studies. But in between, he discusses what he calls the appetitive powers of the soul. The four articles devoted to these are comparatively brief; they are hardly longer than the single article seventy-nine. We will therefore treat them together in this chapter.

In Aquinas' system the intellect and the will are the two great powers of the mind. The intellect is a power of knowing, of a specifically human kind; but it is not the only such power, for there are other ways of acquiring knowledge, such as the senses of sight and hearing which animals have no less than humans. Similarly, the will is a power of wanting, of a specifically human kind; but it is not the only such power, for there are other forms of wanting, such as the appetites which humans share with animals, like hunger and thirst. The will is the power to have wants which only the intellect can frame. It does not take any intellectual ability to desire a plate of meat in front of one; but only an intellectual being can want to worship God or square the circle. If we leave aside the question whether there are non-human intelligences, we can say roughly that the human will is the power to have those wants which only a language-user can have.

The operation of the will is only one kind of wanting, for there is also animal desire; but wanting itself, according to Aquinas, is only one instance of a more general phenomenon, which he calls *appetitus* or tendency. Heavy bodies, if unsupported, will fall; a fire once started and not checked will spread. Aquinas describes these familiar facts by saying that heavy bodies have a natural tendency to fall, and that a fire has a natural tendency to spread.

Wanting, whether animal or human, he regards as a higher analogue of such tendencies. Wanting is a tendency which, unlike
natural tendencies, is dependent upon consciousness.

> Every form is accompanied by some propensity: thus matter
> under the form of fire has a propensity to rise and to propagate
> itself . . . . In things which lack consciousness, there is just the
> single form making each of them the thing it is in accordance
> with its nature; and the natural propensity which accompanies
> the natural form is called a natural tendency. But things which
> have consciousness, beside being determined by their natural
> form to the kind of existence natural to them, can also receive
> forms from other things. The senses receive all sensory forms or
> ideas, the intellect receives the ideas of all thinkable things, so
> that by sense and intellect the human soul is in a manner
> everything.
>
> $(S\ 1,80,1c)^1$

Because they in some manner possess the forms of things other
than themselves, animals and humans have tendencies associated
with the forms of other objects, as well as having the natural
tendencies appropriate to their own form or nature. This does not
mean – as Aquinas will explain later – that an animal inevitably
wants everything it sees, or a human being inevitably wants everything thought of. It is a difference between natural and appetitive
tendencies that the latter are not automatic in their operation. But
the appetitive power of the soul can be defined as the ability to
tend towards objects of awareness ($S\ 1,80,1$).

Because a human being is an animal and not a pure intelligence,
there are in human beings two different appetitive powers, corresponding to the difference between sensory awareness and intellectual understanding. 'Because what is grasped by the intellect is
different in kind from what is grasped by the senses, the intellectual appetite is therefore a different power from the sensory
appetite' ($S\ 80,2c$ and *ad* 1). The sensory appetite is the capacity
for those desires and revulsions which humans and animals have in
common; the intellectual appetite, which is more commonly called
'the will', is the capacity for the kind of wanting that, in this world
at least, is peculiar to language-users.

There are two difficulties about the way in which Aquinas
introduces the notion of appetite. One is that the analogy between
natural tendencies and conscious wanting is unhelpful because of

the archaic physics which lies behind it. According to the post-Aristotelian physics which he accepted, heavy bodies fall, and fire rises, in pursuit of a goal, namely arriving at the place where it is natural for them to be in a fully ordered cosmos. All action, including the most elemental actions of completely inanimate bodies, was for him fundamentally teleological. This part of Aquinas' system is something which must be discarded if we are to make any use of his philosophy at the present time.

But we must make precise what it is we are discarding. It would be wrong to think that when Aquinas attributes ends or aims to inanimate objects, he is being anthropomorphic, or even zoomorphic. He is not attributing to stocks and stones ghostly half-conscious purposes; he insists that inanimate objects have no consciousness. He is perfectly right to insist that teleological activities can take place in the absence of consciousness: the vital activities of plants, which he does not mention in this context, provide a good example. He is also right that inanimate objects have tendencies, and exhibit these tendencies in their natural agency. We can no longer offer earth and air and fire as examples of natural agents, but the action of aqua regia on gold, or of hydrochloric acid on litmus paper are genuine actions of inanimate agents, not just things that happen to those substances. And the notions of natural agency and natural tendency are conceptually linked to each other.

Where Aquinas goes wrong is in thinking that all natural agency is teleological: that is to say, that every natural action is the exercise of a tendency to produce some good (whether it be a good of the agent itself, or a contribution to some overall cosmic beauty). The vital actions of plants are for the good of plants, whether as individuals or as a species; and this remains true even if there is a further, non-teleological, evolutionary explanation of the existence and development of species of teleological agents. But the operation of the laws of inertia and gravity and the natural activities of sulphur or uranium are not teleological activities at all. If we today are to seek, as Aquinas did, to locate animal desire and human willing in a hierarchy of different kinds of tendencies towards good, then we must put at the bottom level of the hierarchy not the natural agency of inanimate matter, but the non-conscious teleological activities to be found in the plant world.

The second difficulty in Aquinas' initial account of appetition is set out clearly by Aquinas himself:

Intellectual awareness is concerned with universals, and this is what distinguishes it from sensory awareness, which is of individuals. But this distinction cannot apply in the appetitive part of the soul. For any wanting is a tendency which moves from the soul towards things; and since things are all individual, every want seems to be a want for an individual thing. So there should not be a distinction made between the intellectual appetite and the sensory appetite.

$(S\ 1,80,2,2)^2$

In reply to this, Aquinas recalls that the will is a power for wanting immaterial goods, such as science and virtue. But his principal answer is that though the will is indeed directed upon individual extra-mental things, it is directed towards them as answering to some universal description. He quotes Aristotle in the *Rhetoric* – 'we hate the whole class of brigands' – as illustrating how a volitional attitude such as hatred can be concerned with something universal.

The point he is making can be put slightly differently. If we express a want in language – say, by giving an order to a waiter – then what eventually satisfies the want will be an individual thing: the particular medium rare steak which he brings. But the initial want was not a want *for that particular steak*. I can complain to the waiter that it is not *the kind of steak* I wanted: I ordered one that was well done. But I cannot complain that I wanted not this individual steak, but a different one exactly like it. In that sense, a want expressed in language can be a universal one, even though it is satisfied by a particular thing. And we might contrast this case with that of two dogs fighting each other over the very same bone (*S* 1,81,2c).

This contrast illustrates the difference between intellectual and sensory appetite even when what is wanted is the same, namely a piece of meat. However, there remains some unclarity in the distinction between the two faculties. Sensual desire can surely not be defined simply as any tendency arising from sense-perception (*S* 1,81,2c). If a collector sees a majolica bowl at an auction and covets it, the desire arises from sense-perception, and yet it may be a highly intellectual desire.

Should we say that the tendency arising from the sense-perception must be a desire for gratification of the perceiving sense? This would mean that the desire to go on gazing at the bowl, as opposed to the desire to add it to one's collection, would be an activity of the sensory appetite. However, this does not seem to be what Aquinas has in mind either. On the contrary, he says this:

> Each power of the soul is itself a form or nature, and has its own natural propensity. Thus it tends, by a natural tendency, towards its appropriate object. The animal desire accompanying awareness is something over and above this. It is not a matter of something being sought as appropriate for the activity of one or other power, sights for seeing and sounds for hearing, but rather as beneficial for the animal itself.
>
> $(S\ 1,80,1\ ad\ 3)^3$

To reconcile the various things Aquinas says we have to say something like this. Not all tendencies arising from sense-perception count as operations of the sensory appetite, but only those which are tendencies to perform specific activities. The desire to eat, the desire to drink, the desire to couple with a perceived object: these are paradigm exercises of the animal appetite. But Aquinas also sees the flight of the sheep from the wolf, and the charge of the enraged bull, as manifestations of appetite. There are negative as well as positive appetitions. Indeed, Aquinas divides the sensory appetite into two sub-faculties: one which is the locus of affective drives, and another which is the locus of aggressive drives. It would be unprofitable to follow in detail his justification for this anatomizing; it consists largely of forced assimilation of diverse classifications made by previous philosophers and theologians.[4]

Altogether, it cannot be said that Aquinas' treatment of sensory desire is quite coherent. In effect, there seem to be several different criteria for a want's being a sensory want. One, the official one, is that it should be a want arising from sense-perception. But this criterion is both too broad and too narrrow to demarcate the class of desires that Aquinas appears to be interested in. On the one hand, it will include the desires of the art-collector, which are intellectual and not sensual; on the other hand, it will exclude hunger, in the case where hunger does not arise from, but precedes, the sight or smell of food in the vicinity.

One might try a different criterion, and say that sensory wants are wants for sense-gratification. Hunger and thirst can be thought of as desires for the pleasures of taste and fulfilment, and sexual drives as desires for the tactile pleasures of intercourse. Because taste and touch are themselves senses, the desire for specific activities of taste and touch can for that reason be called sensory desires. But the use of this criterion will rule out many things which Aquinas sees as manifestations of animal appetite, such as the flight of the lamb and the charge of the bull.

A third criterion which might be used to distinguish sensory wants is to say that they are wants which are themselves feelings. Hunger, thirst and sexual desire are feelings; they are felt desires, desires for gratification *now*, desires with a characteristic pattern of increase prior to satisfaction. They are as much part of our conscious experience as the sights we see and the sounds we hear. This can be a reason for saying that they belong to the sensory and not the intellectual part of the soul. Fear and rage are feelings too, and so this criterion will allow the fear of the lamb, and the rage of the bull, to be exercises of appetite. On the other hand, the desire for a work of art, intense though it may be, is not in the same way a bodily feeling.

These feelings are all associated with tendencies of a particular kind, and indeed we classify feelings as being of one kind rather than another precisely because of the tendencies associated with them. But when we act to gratify a felt desire we are not necessarily acting out a 'tendency arising from sense-awareness', as we should be according to Aquinas' official definition. For hunger, thirst, fear and rage are not themselves forms of awareness (as Aquinas himself insists at *S* 1,81,1) and, as I have already said, they do not necessarily arise from sense-awareness of the objects which would gratify them. What is true is that any such desire involves an awareness of what kind of thing would gratify it, even if only the inchoate awareness of a Cherubino who feels the need to ask his elders what kind of thing love really is.

In the third article of question eighty-one, which is the most interesting article of the question, Aquinas inquires whether the sensitive appetite is or is not obedient to reason. In favour of a negative answer Aquinas puts forth both theological and philosophical arguments. The theological argument is the preacher's text from the Epistle to the Romans: I see another law in my members, warring against the law of my mind, and bringing me into captivity (7,23). The philosophical argument is that the sensitive appetite is a faculty of the sensory part of the soul, just as the senses are; but the senses do not obey reason – seeing and hearing things is not something we can do at will – why then should sensory desires?

Aquinas' response is that the sensory appetite has a twofold subjection to the intellectual part of the soul. First, whereas in animals appetite follows instinct – it is thus that the lamb fears the wolf – in humans desire and fear may be the result of experience and inductive reasoning. Moreover, he says, fear and anger may be augmented or diminished by reflection on general truths. He is presumably thinking of considerations such as 'No son should ever speak to his father in that tone of voice!' or 'Lightning never strikes twice in the same place'. So in these two ways human passions are under the influence of reason.

But there is a second way in which, in humans, desires are subjected to reason. It is not just that reason may cause or control the occurrence of a desire; more than that, whether or not we act upon a felt desire is something which is under the command of the intellectual part of the soul; it is under the influence of the will.

> In other animals the appetite of desire or aggression is acted upon immediately; thus a sheep, in fear of a wolf, runs away immediately, for it has no higher appetite to intervene. But a human being does not react immediately in response to an aggressive or impulsive drive, but waits for the command of a higher appetite, the will.
>
> $(S\ 1,81,3)^5$

Despite the reference to 'waiting for a command', the contrast between immediate and non-immediate reaction is not meant to be taken as a contrast between two different temporal sequences of events. The human shepherd pursued by the wolf may take to his heels just as swiftly as the terrified lamb. But in his case the action is one for which he may be called upon to give reasons; it is an action taken in awareness of the rational considerations for and against it. Because of this, though the fleeing lamb will not be praised or blamed for what he did, the fleeing human may, in appropriate circumstances, be condemned as a bad shepherd.

Though the sensory appetite is subject to the reason, it can disobey reason, as a subject can disobey his ruler. Aquinas sets beside his text from St Paul a text from Aristotle's *Politics*. 'We may observe in living creatures', said Aristotle, 'both a tyrannical and a constitutional rule; for the soul rules the body with a tyrannical rule, while the intellect rules the appetites with a constitutional and royal rule' (*Politics* 1,1254b3–6). Aquinas comments as follows:

> The soul is said to rule the body tyrannically: the bodily parts cannot resist the soul's command, but hand and foot and any other organ naturally subject to voluntary motion move immediately as the soul desires. But intellect and reason rule our appetites like a constitutional monarch, since the sensory appetite has a domain of its own in which it can resist the command of reason. The sensory appetite answers not only to instinct (as in other animals) and not only to inductive generalization (in humans) but also to imagination and sensation. And so we experience conflict between our aggressive or affective appetites and our reason, when we feel or imagine a pleasure reason forbids or a pain reason commands. Conflict in particular cases between reason and appetite is not incompatible with overall obedience.
>
> (*S* 1,82 *ad* 2)[6]

Questions eighty-two and eighty-three are devoted to the topic of the freedom of the will. There is no Latin expression which corresponds exactly to the English expression 'freedom of the will', and of the two questions the first is entitled 'Of the will' (*De voluntate*) and the second 'Of free decision' (*De libero arbitrio*). In a sense the topics discussed throughout are different aspects of the freedom of the will, but the first two articles concern the relationship between will and necessity. The first asks whether the will is ever subject to necessity, and the second asks whether the will is always subject to necessity.

Inevitably, the first step in answering the questions is to make a distinction between different kinds of necessity.

> Something is necessary if it cannot be otherwise. Necessity may arise from something internal, whether material (as when we say that a compound of conflicting elements will necessarily decompose) or formal (as when we say that the three angles of a triangle necessarily equal two right angles). This kind of necessity is natural and absolute necessity. But the impossibility of an alternative may be due to an intrinsic cause, whether final or efficient. Necessity may be imposed by a final cause, in the case where there is something without which a particular goal cannot be achieved, or satisfactorily achieved; as food is necess-

ary for survival, and a horse may be necessary for a journey. This kind of necessity belongs to what is needed, or at least useful, as a means to an end. Necessity may be imposed by an efficient cause, as when an external agent applies force so that one cannot act otherwise. Necessity of this type is called coercion.

(*S* 1,82c)[7]

The different types of necessity are defined by Aquinas in accordance with the schematism of Aristotle's four causes, formal, material, efficient and final.But the same types of necessity are familiar to modern philosophers, who give them names not too different from those used by Aquinas. The necessity of a geometrical theorem is (in a broad sense) logical necessity; the necessity by which radioactive elements decay is physical necessity; the means which are inescapable if a goal is to be achieved are the necessary conditions of that goal; and, like Aquinas, modern philosophers and lawyers will speak of coercion when one human being exercises on another overpowering physical compulsion.

Now, which of these forms of necessity is compatible with the freedom of the will? In the case of two forms of necessity, the answer is easy. First, coercion and voluntariness are incompatible; a coerced act is not something which has its origin in any tendency of the coerced agent's will. Second, the necessity imposed by need is not incompatible with voluntariness. My boarding a ship may be voluntary, even though boarding a ship is a necessary condition of crossing the sea. The necessity of choosing this means is a consequence of the choice to make the voyage. So it is a necessity imposed by the will itself, the willing of the end which involves the willing of the necessary means.

More controversial is the answer to the question whether in the operation of the will there is any room for natural necessity.

Just as the intellect necessarily assents to the first principles of thought, so the will necessarily assents to the pursuit of our ultimate goal of happiness; as Aristotle says in *Physics* II, the goal has the same role in practical reasoning as premises have in theoretical reasoning.

(*S* 1,82c)[8]

Aquinas accepts that this is a limitation on human freedom. The freedom of our will is essentially a freedom of choice; and choice is essentially concerned with means, not ends. Hence the pursuit of an ultimate end is not one of the activities over which human beings are sovereign (*S* 82,1,3 and *ad* 3).

In support of this, as we have seen, Aquinas appeals to the authority of Aristotle. More appropriate Aristotelian support could be drawn from the *Nicomachean Ethics*, where we are told that it is for the sake of happiness that we all do everything else we do (1102a3). The interpretation of this text is controverted: if it means literally that every human action is aimed at happiness, it seems inconsistent with things that Aristotle says elsewhere. He does not seem to wish to rule out the possibility of impulsive actions done for fun without any reference to long-term happiness; even though he does seem to exclude the possibility of a plan of life which was an altruistic one in which one's own happiness took second place. But whatever Aristotle may have thought, it does not seem to be true as a matter of fact that all human actions are done for the sake of happiness, and so Aquinas seems here to be wrongly accepting a limitation on human freedom.

It might be thought that this is merely a matter of words. Aristotle and Aquinas are well aware that human beings may have the most varied and bizarre notions of what happiness is; hence, surely, they will be prepared to call 'the pursuit of happiness' whatever overarching goal individuals set for themselves. So the limitation on liberty is only a verbal one.

But this is not so. First of all, for Aristotle it is only the pursuit of self-regarding goals which count as the pursuit of happiness: the pursuit of one's own good, rather than that of the country, or the party, or the human race. Second, it is a fact, whether or not it is regrettable, that many human actions are not done in pursuit of any overarching goal at all, whether altrustic or egoistic. One may blow bubbles in an idle moment, without having a plan of life in which bubble-blowing has its assigned place. Perhaps Aquinas would save his Aristotelian thesis by maintaining that such idle frivolity is not really an exercise of the will which is the intellectual appetite. If so, then one cannot assume that his theory of the will is an adequate account of human freedom. For spontaneous, purposeless actions are undoubtedly voluntary, and might even be thought to be a particularly striking manifestation of the freedom of the will.

Aquinas' treatment of the freedom of the will – of the extent to which the will escapes necessity – is given in the second article of the question, and it is very much governed by the eudaimonism of the first article.

> There are some objects of thought which have no necessary connection with first principles: contingent propositions which can be denied without entailing any contradiction of first principles. When the intellect assents to these it does not do so of necessity. But there are propositions which are necessary propositions, because they are necessarily connected with first principles: provable conclusions which cannot be denied without entailing a contradiction of first principles. To these the intellect assents of necessity, once their necessary connection with first principles has been deductively proved. But it is not necessitated to assent before it has the necessity of the connection proved to it.
>
> It is the same with the will. There are some particular goods which have no necessary connection with happiness because a human being can be happy without them; nothing necessitates the will to want these. There are other things which do have a necessary connection with happiness, the things that unite men to God in whom alone true happiness is to be found. But until the necessity of this link is established by the vision of God, the will is not necessitated either to want God or the things of God.
>
> (*S* 1,82,2c)[9]

The parallel is beautifully structured. Just as only necessary truths constrain the intellect, so only necessary goods constrain the will. Truths are necessary by formal necessity (as following from first principles), goods are necessary by the necessity of the final cause (as leading to the ultimate end). Yet we may question not only the parallelism, but the description of each side of the parallel.

First of all, is it true that only necessary truths constrain the intellect? It may be true that the intellect cannot but assent to a self-evident truism, to something which, as Descartes would say, I clearly and distinctly perceive. But are there not also contingent truths that I cannot sincerely deny? If I see my mother in plain view just in front of me, am I at liberty to believe that she is not there? Can I really suspend my belief that Great Britain is an island?

On the other side of the parallel, is it not possible to believe that something is necessary for one's happiness, and yet renounce it –

whether for good or bad reasons? A wife may be convinced that she will never be happy unless she leaves her husband, and yet stay with him for the sake of the children. On the other hand, the mere fact that a particular good is not necessarily connected with happiness is not enough to establish my freedom not to choose it. If I am a chain-smoker who gets through a hundred cigarettes a day, am I free at any moment to stop smoking? Perhaps I am: but to prove that I am, it is not sufficient to point out that human beings can be happy without smoking at all.

Finally, there seems to be a flaw in the parallel between following from first principles and leading to an ultimate end. Whatever follows from necessary truths is itself necessary; but it is not the case that whatever leads to a necessary end is itself necessary. So that even if we accept that humans cannot but have the goal of happiness, it does not follow that there is anything which is necessary for happiness: there may be many, different, incompatible ways of achieving happiness. Of course Aquinas believed that ultimate happiness was only to be found in God, and that God had laid down certain necessary requirements which men had to fulfil if they were to find Him. But this means that Aquinas' account of necessity and liberty in the will needs a theological context which was not needed for his account of necessity and liberty in the intellect.

In the objections and answers to the article, however, Aquinas gives two grounds for the freedom of the will which do not set its bounds within theological limits. In the second argument for the necessity of the will, it is argued that the will has the same relation to its object as a moving body has to what is moving it. One might have expected a response to the effect that a mover acts by efficient causality, while an object of desire acts by final causality. But that would not suffice, since Aquinas believes that final causality can be necessitating no less than efficient causality. Instead the answer is given that an efficient cause only causes movement or change of necessity if its power to cause change is greater than the power to resist change in the object affected. But the will's power extends to universal and total good, and therefore no particular good can exhaust it. No particular good, however great, can take away the will's power to want something different. This picture of the will is a rather different one from the eudaimonistic one; reminiscent of Sartre rather than of Aristotle.

The second argument for the necessity of the will goes as

follows. What is perceived by sense necessarily arouses the sensory appetite, therefore what is grasped by the intellect necessarily brings the intellectual appetite into operation. The response does not question the description of sensory appetite, but explains that while each of the senses is only aware of one aspect of things, the reason is aware of many aspects, any one of which may sway the will. This multi-faceted nature of practical reason is something which is given large scope elsewhere in Aquinas' treatment of the freedom of the will.

Article three of question eighty-two inquires which is the higher power, the intellect or the will. This kind of inquiry is likely to seem uninviting to modern philosophers, who find strange the idea of a kind of spiritual beauty contest in which prizes are awarded to faculties or virtues on a scale of nobility. But the article addresses issues which have struck a chord in thinkers of different ages and kinds, from the author of the *Imitation of Christ*, who remarked famously 'I had rather feel remorse than know its definition', to Karl Marx, who complained that philosophers had only interpreted the world, when the point was to change it. Both these utterances assign a certain primacy to the will over the intellect; and in this article Aquinas asks whether this is the correct attitude.

From Aquinas' standpoint, the strongest argument for the primacy of the will comes from Scripture. St Paul said: 'If I were to know all mysteries and to have all faith, but not have charity, I am nothing.' But charity is a matter of the will, whereas knowledge is in the intellect. So the will is above the intellect. Against this, Aristotle stated flatly that the intellect was the highest part of the soul.

The apparent conflict between these august authorities must be settled, naturally, by making distinctions which will show that they are both in the right.

If we consider intellect and will simply as faculties, the intellect is superior. Both of them are concerned with goodness: but while the will can want various concrete goods, the intellect can achieve a general theory of goodness. The intellect does not just identify and pursue goods, but can explain in what their goodness consists and why they should be pursued.

But though the intellect as a faculty is superior to the will as a faculty, there may be particular activities of the will which are superior to any acts of the intellect. Aquinas explains how this can be (*S* 1,82,3):

The activity of the intellect consists in the existence in the thinker of the concept of what is thought about; but the upshot of the activity of the will is the will's tending towards the extramental reality as it is in itself. For this reason, Aristotle says in *Metaphysics* VI that good and evil (the objects of the will) are in things, while truth and falsehood (the objects of the intellect) are in the mind. So when the bearer of goodness is more noble than the mind thinking the concept of it, the volition for such an object is superior to the thought of it; but when the bearer of goodness is inferior to the soul, then the thought of such an object is superior to the volition for it. Hence, the love of God is better than the knowledge of God; but the knowledge of bodily things is better than the love of them.[10]

Aristotle's dictum that good and evil are in things, while truth and falsehood are in the mind, may seem hard to understand. It has been well paraphrased by Professor Anscombe, in her book *Intention* (Anscombe, 1957,75):

The conceptual connexion between 'wanting' . . . and 'good' can be compared to the conceptual connexion between 'judgment' and 'truth'. Truth is the object of judgment, and good the object of wanting; it does not follow from this either that everything judged must be true, or that everything wanted must be good. But there is a certain contrast between these pairs of concepts too. For you cannot explain truth without introducing as its subject intellect, or judgment, or propositions, in some relation of which to the things known or judged truth consists; 'truth' is ascribed to what has the relation, not to the things. With 'good' and 'wanting' it is the other way round; an account of 'wanting' introduces good as its object, and goodness of one sort or another is ascribed primarily to the objects, not to the wanting: one wants a *good kettle*, but has a *true idea* of a kettle (as opposed to wanting a kettle well, or having an idea of a true kettle).

The comparison and contrast between the will and the intellect is carried further in the fourth article of question eighty-two. Here the question is whether the will moves the intellect: that is to say, whether the intellect is under voluntary control. But the answer spells out the interlocking relationships between the two.

In one sense, it is the intellect which brings the will into play.

For the will can only want something to the extent that the want can be formulated: the good aimed at must be specified. And formulating the want and specifying the target good are intellectual operations. In this sense, Aquinas says, 'the good thought of is the object of the will and acts upon it as an end'.

In another sense, it is the will which sets the intellect to act. The operation of our intellectual faculties, unlike the operation of our digestion, is something subject to voluntary control. It is up to us what we think about.

Each of the two faculties has the other within its ambit. The intellect can think about the will, and the will's activities and objects, no less than about material objects like stocks and stones. On the other hand, the operation of the intellect is one among the many possible goods which may be objects of volition: we can want to understand, and we can want to attain to truth. So the activities and objects of intellect and will mutually include each other: the intellect understands the will's willing, and the will wills the intellect's understanding. There are truths about goodness which the intellect understands, and one of the goods at which the will aims is truth.

Is there a danger of an endless regress here? Aquinas raises the question himself:

> We cannot want anything unless we think of it. So if the will moves the intellect to think by willing to think, that willing will have to be preceded by another thought, and that thought by another willing, and so on *ad infinitum*. But that is impossible; so the will does not move the intellect.
>
> $(S\ 1,82,4,3)$[11]

Aquinas replies that though every volition requires thought, not every thought is voluntary. Hence, there is no regress; but of course the question remains: what is the cause of non-voluntary thought? And the ultimate answer to that question, Aquinas says with an allusion to a mysterious passage in Aristotle's *Eudemian Ethics*, is God.[12]

6 The freedom of the will

Question eighty-three, like question eighty-two, is devoted to the question of whether human beings are free. But the question is discussed with a different repertoire of concepts. In English it is natural to phrase the question of human freedom in the terms: do human beings have free will? But there is no expression in Aquinas' Latin which corresponds exactly to the English 'free will'. Aquinas speaks of the will (*voluntas*); that is the intellectual appetite which was the subject of question eighty-two. But he does not customarily speak of free will (*libera voluntas*) or of the freedom of the will (*libertas voluntatis*). The noun which goes with the Latin word for 'free' is not 'will' but 'decision' (*arbitrium*). It is to the topic of free decision, *liberum arbitrium*, that question eighty-three is devoted.

In the two successive articles, Aquinas presents essentially the same theory in two different terminologies. The reasons for the duplication of concepts is historical. The discussion of the will derives from the philosophical tradition going back to Aristotle. The discussion of free choice harks back to the theological controversy between St Augustine and his Pelagian opponents concerning the relation between human freedom and divine grace.

The theological setting of the discussion is made clear at the outset by the arguments presented in the first article in favour of denying freedom of decision. These arguments amount to a list of Scripture texts stressing human helplessness and the power of God. They are texts familiar in controversies about grace from the time of Augustine onwards and especially in the period of the Reformation, such as 'It is not of him that willeth, nor of him that runneth, but of God that sheweth mercy' from St Paul's Epistle to the Romans (9,16), and 'It is God which worketh in you both to will and to do of his good pleasure', from the Epistle to the Philippians (2,13). As a rebuttal of these texts, Aquinas quotes from the Apocrypha: 'In the beginning God made man and left him in the hands of his own counsel' (Ecclesiasticus 15,14).

The substantial argument in favour of the existence of freedom is brief. If humans were not free in their decisions, there would be no point in advice, encouragement, commands and prohibitions, rewards and punishments. Freedom of decision, Aquinas continues, is implicit in the notion of rational agency.

> Agents without consciousness act without judgement, in the way that stones fall to earth. Some agents, such as dumb animals, act upon judgement, but not free judgement. A sheep seeing a wolf judges by natural judgement, not free judgement, that flight is appropriate; it makes the judgement by natural instinct, not by weighing arguments, and that is how it is with all animal judgement. But human beings make up their own minds and judge on the basis of experience whether something is to be avoided or pursued. And because a particular practical evaluation is not a matter of inborn instinct, but a result of weighing reasons, a human being acts upon free judgement, and is capable of going various ways. In contingent matters reason can go either way . . . and what to do in particular situations is a contingent matter. So in such cases the judgement of reason is open to alternatives and is not determined to any one course. Hence, humans enjoy free decision, from the very fact of being rational.
>
> $(S\ 1,83,1c)^1$

This passage links together the discussion of *liberum arbitrium* with the theory of will as intellectual appetite. If the will is a rational appetite, an ability to have reasons for acting and to act for reasons, then the nature of the will must depend on the nature of practical reasoning. In practical reasoning the relationship between premises and conclusion is not as tight or as easy to regiment as that between premises and conclusion in theoretical reasoning. When we look at a piece of practical reasoning – reasoning about what to do – we often appear to find, where the analogy of theoretical reasoning would lead us to expect necessitation, merely contingent and defeasible connections between one step and another. Aquinas believed that the peculiar contingency of practical reasoning was an essential feature of the human will as we know it. Here and elsewhere he states this contingency as being the fundamental ground of human freedom.

In answering the theological difficulties, Aquinas maintains that free decision and divine grace are not competing explanations of human conduct. Man's decision and God's help may both be necessary for effective action. Freedom is self-determination, but self-determination is compatible with determination by God.

> By free decision a human being moves himself into action; but it is not essential to freedom that the free agent should be its own first cause, just as in general to be the cause of something one does not have to be its first cause. God is the first cause which activates both natural and voluntary causes. His action on natural causes does not prevent their activities from being natural; equally, in activating voluntary causes he does not take away the voluntariness of their actions. On the contrary, it is he who makes their actions voluntary; for he works in each thing in accord with its own characteristics.
>
> $(S\ 1,83\ ad\ 3)$[2]

Philosophers who, like St Thomas, believe in the freedom of the will are commonly called libertarians. Many libertarians would find it difficult to accept the assumptions of the paragraph just quoted. For many, perhaps most, libertarians regard it as an essential element of free action that it should be uncaused, whereas in this passage, St Thomas seems to be denying the possibility of contra-causal freedom. It is necessary, he says, for free action that the agent should be a cause, and a special kind of cause, of action; but it is not necessary, apparently, that he should be the only cause. Self-determination is essential; but it is compatible with divine determination.

Hence, Aquinas appears to believe that freedom is compatible with some sorts of determinism. Many philosophers have concurred with him in this: such philosophers are nowadays called compatibilists. A compatibilist need not be a determinist: she may or may not believe that determinism is actually true. If a compatibilist believes that it is untrue, she will also believe that even if were true, that would not necessarily rule out freedom. A compatibilist who does believe in some sort of determinism is commonly called a 'soft' determinist (as opposed to a 'hard' determinist, who believes not only that determinism is true but also that free will is an illusion). In the contemporary terminology, Aquinas is a soft determinist: he believes that human beings are free in their actions, but he also believes that they are determined to act by God.

There are other forms of determinism besides theological determinism, and in this article Aquinas considers some of them: psychological and physiological determinism. Some determinists believe that human action is determined by psychological and physiological factors which are outside the agent's conscious control. This type of determinism is enunciated in the fifth objection which Aquinas brings against the doctrine of free choice. Aristotle, he says there, taught that the goals we pursue are determined by the kind of persons we are. But it is not in our power to be a particular kind of person; we are made the kind of people we are by nature. So it is nature, and not free decision, which determines our goals (*S* 1,83,1,5).

In reply to this Aquinas makes one concession to psychological determinism. As we have seen, he believes that by nature we all seek happiness, and that the pursuit of happiness is something which is beyond the scope of free decision. But he denies that any characteristic of an individual, whether inborn or acquired, takes away freedom of choice.

> As to the body and its powers, a person can be endowed with natural qualities of constitution or temperament as a result of the operation of all kinds of physical causes; but these cannot determine the operation of the intellectual part, because that is not the activity of anything bodily. The sense in which it is true that the goals we pursue are determined by our physical constitution is that our temperament inclines us to choose certain things and reject others. But such inclinations are subject to the judgement of reason, which controls the lower appetites, as has been said. So this leaves the freedom of decision intact.
>
> (*S* 1,83,2 *ad* 5)[3]

The crucial, and questionable, point here is the statement that the operation of the intellect can escape the determinism which rules in the body, because it is not itself the activity of anything bodily. This is a point to which we shall have to return when we have followed Aquinas' fuller account of the relationship between the mind and the brain. Elsewhere, St Thomas in addressing this question makes use of the Aristotelian distinction between natural and voluntary causes. A natural cause, unlike a voluntary cause, is 'determined to one thing' (*S* 1–2, 50,3). That is to say, in the order of nature, if the causal conditions in a situation can be fully specified, a single effect can be infallibly predicted. In the order of voluntary behaviour, it is not so: when a man does something, for instance, because he is asked to, his doing it cannot be predicted infallibly even by somebody who knows everything that has been said by him and to him throughout his life up to the request itself. This distinction seems to me both correct and important. Of course, it does not solve, but only sharpen, the problem of free will. Natural effects can be predicted from natural causes, voluntary effects cannot be predicted from voluntary causes. Just so: but voluntary actions are also natural events, and the interesting and difficult question is whether voluntary effects can be predicted from natural causes. It is sufficient to note now that St Thomas is prepared to agree that our likes and dislikes, below the strictly intellectual level of the operation of the will, can be the consequences of physical causes, whether they are inborn or acquired. However, they can be controlled by the dictate of reason. Our virtues and vices, he goes on to say, are also voluntary in the sense that it is up to us whether we acquire them or prevent ourselves from acquiring them. So here too there is no threat to free will.

The remaining three articles of question eighty-three are concerned with tidying up the terminology used by different authors in discussing human freedom. There seems to be a difficulty in identifying *voluntas* and *liberum arbitrium* because the will is a faculty, and decision seems to be a particular action or event. He explains that when writers talk of 'free decision' in this context, they mean not the act of deciding, but what makes free decision possible. In theory, this might be an acquired disposition (in the way in which the acquired virtue of courage makes courageous acts possible). But freedom could not be a disposition: it could not be a natural disposition, because what we are disposed to naturally is not under our control, so that freedom itself would be unfree; and it could not be an acquired disposition, because we are free by nature, and acquired dispositions make us tend one way or another, whereas freedom is the ability to go either way. Hence what makes free decision possible is not a disposition, but a faculty: the very same faculty, in fact, as the will (*S* 1,83,2).

There is a further terminological difficulty. As we have seen, Aquinas, in explaining freedom of decision, constantly appealed to the freedom of the judgements occurring in practical reasoning.

But judgement seems to be a cognitive, not an appetitive act, and reasoning is surely an operation of the intellect, not of the will. Aquinas deals with this difficulty by appealing to the Aristotelian analysis of the key notion of choice. What makes us free is that we can take one thing while rejecting another, that is to say, make choices.

> Choice is a combination of a cognitive and an appetitive element. On the cognitive side, it involves deliberation, by which we discern what is to be preferred to what; on the appetitive side, it involves an attitude of assent to what is discerned by deliberation . . . . What choice is specifically concerned with is means to an end; and a means is something which bears a specific kind of goodness, namely usefulness. Since good is the object of appetitive powers, it follows that choice is primarily an act of appetition, and that freedom of choice is an appetitive power.
>
> (*S* 1,83,3c)[4]

Aquinas makes reference to a famous passage in the sixth book of the *Nicomachean Ethics*, where Aristotle says that the origin of conduct is choice, and the origin of choice is appetition plus means–end reasoning; reasoning by itself moves nothing, only means–end reasoning concerned with good conduct which is the end of appetition. The passage concludes 'Therefore choice is either appetitive intelligence or ratiocinative appetite' (*NE* 6,1139a30ff.). Aquinas notes that Aristotle here seems uncertain whether to assign choice to the intellect or to the will. Elsewhere, however, he unequivocally describes it as a form of appetition (*NE* 3,1113a9–12), and this is the position Aquinas accepts.

In the *Ethics* Aristotle also makes a distinction between wish (*boulesis*) and choice (*prohairesis*): wish relates to the end, choice to the means to the end; we wish to be healthy, but we choose what will lead to health; we wish to be happy, but we cannot choose to be happy. The Greek word commonly translated into English as 'wish' appears in the Latin translation as the same word as 'will'. Accordingly, Aquinas accepts it as Aristotle's view that willing concerns the end, and choice concerns the means. Does it follow, then, that freedom of choice is something different from the will (*S* 1,83,4,2)?

Aquinas responds by drawing up the parallel between the cognitive and appetitive faculties of the mind. The activity of the intellect is *intelligere*, to understand; but there is understanding in the broad sense of thinking, which includes reasoning, and there is understanding in the narrow sense which is the grasp of self-evident principles. As understanding is to reasoning, so willing is to choice. Willing in the broad sense covers any activity of the will, including choice, but willing in the narrow sense is concerned with ends rather than means.

On the appetitive side, 'to will' indicates the plain wanting of something, so willing is said to be of the end which is wanted for its own sake. To choose, by contrast, is to want something for the sake of achieving something else; hence strictly it concerns means to an end. As on the cognitive side we assent to a conclusion because of the premises, so on the appetitive side we want the means for the sake of the end. So clearly, the relation between the will and the faculty of choice, or free decision, is the same as that between the intellect and the reason. And we showed earlier that understanding and reasoning are both activities of the same faculty (just as a power to move is also a power to stay still). Hence, willing and choosing are activities of the same faculty, and therefore the will and free decision are not two different powers but a single one.

$$(S\ 1,84,4)^5$$

The will, in Aquinas' system, seems to have two different roles. On the one hand, it is a capacity for certain kinds of wanting (for long-term and universal goals that only humans can have, such as the discovery of scientific truth or the pursuit of riches). On the other hand, it is a capacity for action of a certain kind, namely free and voluntary action; only those who have free will are capable of free action. But what is the precise relationship between the possession of intellectual appetite, and the capacity for voluntary action?

The actions of higher animals seem on the face of it to be voluntary; and this is so whether we think that the essence of voluntary action is that it should be action which is wanted by the agent, or whether we think that for an act to be voluntary what is essential is that it should be performed by an agent who can do otherwise. When my dog, instead of coming when I call, chases a cat across the neighbouring field, he is acting as he does because he wants to, and in full possession of the ability to come home instead. Moreover, animals often do one thing for the sake of another: and isn't that a case of choosing means to ends?

Aquinas thinks that the actions of animals are voluntary, but only in a diminished sense of the word (*S* 1–2,6,2). Voluntariness, he says, involves an internal origin for an action, and a degree of knowledge of the end. He goes on:

> There are two kinds of knowledge of the end, perfect and imperfect. Perfect knowledge of an end involves not merely the apprehension of the object which is the end, but an awareness of it precisely qua end, and of the relationship to it of the means which are directed to it. Such a knowledge is within the competence only of a rational nature. Imperfect knowledge of the end is mere apprehension of the end, without any awareness of its nature as an end or of the relationship of the activity to the end. This type of knowledge is found in dumb animals, by sense and instinct.
>
> (*S* 1–2,6,3)[6]

Full-blooded voluntariness, which permits an agent in awareness of an end 'to deliberate about the end and the means, and to pursue it or not to pursue it' accompanies perfect knowledge; imperfect knowledge brings with it only a second-class voluntariness.

Aquinas is not denying that animals act for the sake of ends, or that they are aware of their goals; he is denying that they are aware of them *as goals*. Similarly, he is not denying that they aim at goals by doing things in order to achieve them; but he denies that this is a choice of means to ends. What is the justification for these denials?

When a human being does X in order to do Y, the achieving of Y is his reason for doing X. When an animal does X in order to do Y, he does not do X for a reason, even though he is aiming at a goal in doing so. Since he lacks a language, he cannot give a reason; and only those beings who can give reasons can act for reasons. Humans are rational, reason-giving animals; cats and dogs are not, and therefore cannot act for reasons.

If I run down the road to catch a thief, my wanting to catch the thief is manifested by my running; but it can also be expressed in language in answer to the question 'Why are you running?' This two-tiered possibility of expression is not open to animals, who lack language. When Fido scratches to get at the buried bone, his scratching manifests his desire to get at the bone; and he may well be aware of the bone in the sense that he can smell it. But even though his action is caused by his desire for his goal (the bone), he lacks, in Aquinas' terms, any knowledge of the relationship of the activity to the end (*proportio actus ad finem*). This is because there is nothing in his repertoire to express that he is scratching *because* he wants to get at the bone. Nor is he aware of his goal as a goal; in Aquinas' terms, he lacks the *ratio finis*. Though gnawing bones and sleeping by the fire are both among his ends, he has no means of expressing the possession of a common concept under which both these ends fall. In just the same way, animals, though they possess consciousness, lack self-consciousness. Fido may think there is a bone buried beneath the bush; but unless he has a language, he cannot have the thought that he is thinking that there is a bone buried beneath the bush.

Aquinas does not emphasize, as I do, the importance of language in connection with human willing. None the less, in several places, especially in *De Veritate* (24,2), he makes a close connection between freedom and self-reflection. He says:

> Judgement is in the power of the person judging to the extent that he can make a judgement about his own judging; for whatever is in our power is something we can make a judgement about. But only reason can make a judgement about its own judgement, which reflects upon its own action, and knows the relationships of the things it judges about and the things by which it makes its judgement. Hence, the basis of all freedom is built upon reason.
>
> (*V* 24,2)[7]

Animals, lacking language, lack both self-consciousness and the capacity for rational choice.

Aquinas makes a distinction between two kinds of acts of the will. The exercises of the faculty fall into two classes: *actus eliciti* and *actus imperati* (*S* 1–2,1,1 *ad* 2; 6,4c). *Actus eliciti* he describes as *actus immediati voluntatis*, unmediated acts of the will; he gives as instances such things as enjoying, choosing, deliberating, consenting (*S* 1–2,11–15). *Actus imperati* are 'acts commanded by the will': Aquinas has in mind such things as walking and speaking and other voluntary motions of the body, acts whose execution involves some power other than the will (*S* 1–2,17).

The existence of *actus imperati* is beyond doubt; later, we shall look further at what is meant by saying that such acts as walking and speaking are commanded by the will. But is Aquinas right to think that wherever we have voluntary action there is also an inner act of the will, an *actus elicitus*? Philosophers in several traditions have believed that there are mental events called volitions whose occurrence make the difference between voluntary and involuntary actions. It has been widely believed that for an overt action to be voluntary is for it to be preceded and caused by a characteristic internal impression or conscious thought.

In our own time, this theory has been subject to devastating criticism. In his book *The Concept of Mind* Gilbert Ryle argued that if volitions were genuine mental events occurring with the frequency which this theory demands, it should be possible for any articulate human being to answer questions about their nature, occurrence, timing, intensity and qualities. But it is not difficult to construct a battery of questions on such topics, to which no coherent answers present themselves. Further, Ryle employs a regress argument. Volitions are postulated to be that which makes actions voluntary. But not only bodily, but also mental operations may be voluntary. So what of volitions themselves? Are they voluntary or involuntary motions of the mind? If the latter, then how can the actions that issue from them be voluntary? If the former, then they must themselves proceed from prior volitions, and those from other volitions, and so on *ad infinitum*.

Is Aquinas' system caught by these arguments? Does his acknowledgement of *actus eliciti*, unmediated actualizations of the pure will, make him vulnerable to Ryle's criticisms? Undoubtedly Aquinas believes that whenever voluntary action occurs, an *actus elicitus* is present. If, therefore, by *actus elicitus* he means a phenomenon of consciousness, then he is committed to the objectionable theory of volitions. But is that what he means?

Certainly his teaching is often taken in this sense. Thus Copleston, discussing 'human acts' in Aquinas, acts which proceed from the agent considered precisely as a rational free being, has this to say:

A modern reader might be inclined to understand the word 'act' in this connexion as meaning an action which can in principle be observed by other people, the action, for example, of giving money to a needy person, or the act of stealing jewellery. So it may be as well to remark at once that Aquinas makes a distinction betwen the 'interior act' and the 'exterior act'. Obviously, if we are talking about human acts in the technical sense, there cannot be an exterior act without an interior act; for a human act is defined with reference to the will. In every human act the will is directed towards an end apprehended by the reason. Therefore in every human act there must be an interior act of the will. But there can be an interior act without what would ordinarily be reckoned as the corresponding exterior act. A man might, for instance, make up his mind to steal a watch, though he never actually does so, perhaps because a good opportunity for doing so does not occur. When therefore Aquinas talks about morally good and morally bad acts he refers primarily to interior acts. If, however, the interior act issues in an exterior act or is considered as doing so, the word 'act' signifies the total complex unless some qualification or the context shows that the word is being used in a more restricted sense.[8]

A Rylean philosopher might reply: it is just not the case that the majority of what are normally called human acts – acts for which a person would be held morally or legally responsible – are preceded by an interior act resembling the taking of a decision. So either Aquinas' account of human actions is unclear on a crucial point, or his concept of 'human act' applies only to a small sample of reponsible human behaviour.

But there is reason to doubt whether Copleston gives an accurate interpretation of Aquinas' meaning. It is misleading to take the Latin word *actus* to refer necessarily to an act, whether interior or exterior. The Latin word need not mean any sort of action at all; it is the term for 'actualization' as opposed to 'potentiality'. Being hot or being square would be an *actus*, and neither of these is a momentary episode of the kind suggested by the expression 'interior act'. Aquinas often speaks of an *actus voluntatis*, a volition, as being an *inclinatio*, a tendency or disposition rather than an episode.[9] Such a tendency can be operative without being present to consciousness, as one's desire to reach a destination can govern one's behaviour on a journey without being the object of one's thoughts from moment to moment (*S* 1–2,1,6 *ad* 3).

So when Aquinas says that all properly human actions must issue from a *voluntas deliberata* (*S* 1–2,1,1), he does not mean that they must be preceded and caused by an event of consciousness. But it was that theory that was exploded by Ryle. It would, after all, be surprising if Aquinas could be impaled on Ryle's infinite regress, since he had himself considered and disarmed the regress argument. If volitions are not motions of the mind, but states of mind, it can be allowed that voluntary action is action issuing from a volition, without this having any implication that volitions must be preceded by volitions *ad infinitum*. Volition not being itself an action does not fall under the law that all voluntary action is action issuing from a volition.

When Aquinas says that *actus eliciti* are 'unmediated exercises of the will', he is not referring to mythical acts of pure willing; he means merely that when we describe someone as wanting something, or intending to do something, or delighting in something, we are merely recording the state of his will, and not saying anything about his talents, skills, abilities or the exercises of his other faculties. When Aquinas says that every *actus imperatus* has its origin in an *actus elicitus*, he need mean no more than the truism that if you do something voluntarily you do it because you in some sense *want* to do it.[10]

Of the items called *actus eliciti* by St Thomas, some do seem to be actions in the ordinary sense of clockable voluntary performances: deciding, for instance, which may happen at a particular time, and deliberation, which may last over a period of time. Others, like wanting or intending, are not actions but states. Forming an intention may be a datable event; but not all intentions are formed; that is to say, an intention may be in existence at a certain time without there having been a particular moment at which it came into being.

If *actus eliciti* are pure states of the will, then it seems that Aquinas was misguided in assigning interior actions like deciding and deliberating to this category. Making up one's mind to do something may be an interior act in the sense that it is something that one can do without anyone but onself knowing about it. But it is not something which is a pure exercise of the will. Deliberation involves the use of the imagination, as when, in interior monologue, one weighs up the pros and cons of the proposed course of action. The inward passage from premises to conclusion is an exercise of the reason. The 'exercises of the will' are the appetitive states from which deliberation arises and in which it culminates: according to Aquinas' own account, the initial wanting of the end, and the final wanting of the means in which, via deliberation, it issues.

Deliberation, as Aquinas describes it, seems to be not an *actus elicitus* but an inner *actus imperatus*. Aquinas says that an *actus imperatus* can be impeded by outside forces, but not an *actus elicitus*, because it is contrary to the notion of the will's own act that it should be subject to compulsion or violence. If so, then deliberating cannot be an *actus elicitus*; a blow on the head may interrupt deliberation about how best to steal the jewellery just as it may interrupt the theft itself. Whatever Aquinas may have thought, it seems that all genuine *actus eliciti* – all 'pure actualizations of the will' – are states, and not actions or clockable events with a beginning, a middle and an end. The nearest to a 'pure act of the will' that we can come without falling into nonsense seems to be the onset of a volitional attitude. If I hear of a prospective sharp rise in the value of a certain stock, I may be suddenly smitten with a keen desire to purchase some. Here it is clearly the intellectual and not the sensory appetite that is in play: none the less, the desire may have a sudden onset and perhaps a felt history.

It is time to turn from *actus eliciti* to *actus imperati*. The description of actions as 'commanded by the will' is an invitation to compare the relationship between willing and acting to the relationship between a command and its execution. Talk of 'acts commanded by the will' is clearly metaphorical. It is possible to give commands to oneself: an officer may declare a house out of bounds to all ranks, including himself, and the Pope may impose celibacy on all priests, including himself. But it would be absurd to suggest that in every case of voluntary action there occurs some form of self-command analogous to these cases.

None the less, the metaphor of the will issuing commands is an appropriate one, and the comparison between the relationship of command to execution and the relationship of willing to acting is a fruitful one. A volition, in the case of human beings, is a state of mind which is defined by the linguistic description of the action or state of affairs which would fulfil it. I want it to be the case that p. The propostion p both specifies my state of mind and demarcates the state of affairs that stands to it in the relationship of fulfilment to want. But suppose that instead of my wanting it to be the case that p, you command me to bring it about that p: the proposition p has an analogous role. The relationship between our voluntary actions and our volitions is, formally speaking, the same as that between actions and commands. By acting we carry out, or fulfil, our own volitions, just as by acting we carry out, or fulfil, the commands we are given by others. The relation between a command and its fulfilment, and the relation between an intention and its execution, are both internal, logical, relations. That is to say, the description of the content of the command is the same description as the description of the action which obeys it; the description of the content of an intention is the same description as the description of the action which executes it. It is for this reason that it is illuminating to take the relationship between command and obedience as the paradigm for understanding the nature of volitions in general. That is why Aquinas is well inspired to call voluntary action action that is commanded by the will.[11]

7 Sense, imagination and intellect

Articles eighty-four, eighty-five and eighty-six form, in Aquinas' plan, a unity. They are all concerned with intellectual knowledge of the physical world. The first of the three, question eighty-four, discusses the relationship between the intellect, the senses and the imagination.

When Aquinas treats of intellectual knowledge of the physical world, it is above all natural science whose possibility he is concerned to defend. 'Science is in the intellect', he says in the *sed contra* to the first article, 'so if there is no intellectual knowledge of bodies, there will be no science of bodies. And that will be the end of natural science, whose object is bodies and their changes' (*S* 1,84,1c). The world around us is material and constantly changing; how then can there be immaterial and stable knowledge of it?

Aquinas' preliminary answer is that every change presupposes something unchanging: when something changes colour, the sensory qualities vary, but the substance remains the same substance; when wine turns into vinegar, one substantial form replaces another, but the same matter remains. Changeable things have unchanging relationships. That Socrates is sitting is a contingent truth; that if he is sitting he is not standing is an unchanging truth. It is by grasping unchanging truths about changing objects that physical science is possible (*S* 1,84,1 *ad* 3).

Before setting out his own account of how such knowledge operates, Aquinas sets up for criticism a number of false theories concerning it. Article one is an attack on the materialist theory of knowledge; article three rejects the theory of innate ideas, and article four returns to the criticism of Plato's theory of Ideas.

The crudest form of the materialist theory of knowledge was that developed by some of the Presocratic philosophers on the basis of the slogan that like knows like. In order to know what is material, our minds must share the nature of matter.

> The earliest physicists, starting from the premise that the things known by the soul are corporeal and material, maintained that they must exist in a material way in the knowing soul as well. So in order to allow the soul knowledge of everything, they postulated that it had a nature in common with everything. Because the nature of compounds is determined by their elements, they attributed to the soul the nature of whatever they regarded as elemental: thus, if a philosopher thought that fire was the universal element, he would say that the soul was made of fire; and similarly with air and water.
>
> $$(S\ 1,84,2c)^1$$

In the second article, Aquinas takes a stand against the materialists who argued that if the soul was to know matter it must contain matter, since like can only be known by like. In reply, he draws out into patent nonsense the nonsense that is latent in the materialist position.

If it was necessary, he says, for a thing known to be in the soul materially, then there would be no reason why things which exist materially outside the soul should lack knowledge. Let us suppose that the materialist was right, and it was the presence of actual fire in the soul that explained how the soul could know fire. In that case, why should not fire outside the soul also be conscious of fire?

Modern materialists identify the mind with the brain. They then identify the problem of explaining how the mind knows X with the problem of explaining how X is in the brain – not literally, but in encoded form. Once they have shown that there is an encoding of X in the brain (or, more plausibly, once they have shown that, for all we know, there may be an encoding of X in the brain), they think that they have explained knowledge of X. But in fact the problem remains just where it was: for the problem of knowledge is the problem of what makes a pattern into a code.

Aquinas would say: let us suppose that X itself is present in the brain, and not just in coded form. How does that explain knowledge of X? After all, there is in the brain oxygen itself, and not merely a code for oxygen. But the presence of oxygen in the brain does not explain how a scientist knows what oxygen is. There is oxygen in the brain of many mammals who have not the faintest idea what oxygen is. And if the presence of oxygen explained knowledge of oxygen, then, as Aquinas would say, fire would know what oxygen was.

The account of innate ideas in article three is much less carefully worked out than that in the *Prima Secundae* in the treatment of dispositions, in the first article of question fifty-one. The position which Aquinas takes in the debate about the existence of innate ideas is a balanced one, taking acount of arguments on both sides of the question. There are, he says, no completely innnate dispositions to activity which are present in all members of the human race; but some men, because of the fortunate constitution of their bodies, are born with gifts of intelligence or advantages of temperament which are denied to other men; and these natural endowments are dispositions of a kind (*S* 1–2,51,1). Again, there are no completely innate ideas or beliefs; but belief in self-evident propositions is innate in a specially qualified sense. 'Because of the nature of his spiritual soul', St Thomas tells us, 'a human being, once he knows what a whole is and what a part is, knows that every whole is greater than any of its parts.' But, he continues, a man cannot know what a whole is or what a part is except through the possession of concepts derived through the senses. The understanding of self-evident principles is thus in one sense innate and in another sense acquired by experience (*S* 1–2,51,1).

Plato had maintained, Aquinas says, that the human intellect naturally contained all intelligible ideas, but was prevented from using them because of its union with the body. Against this Aquinas marshals both empirical and metaphysical arguments.

If the soul has a natural knowledge of all these things it does not seem possible that it should so far forget this natural knowledge as to be ignorant that it has it at all. For nobody forgets what he naturally knows, as that the whole is greater than its parts and so on. Plato's theory seems especially unacceptable if the soul is, as maintained above, naturally united to the body; for it is unacceptable that the natural operation of a thing should be altogether impeded by something else which is also natural to it. Secondly, the falsity of this theory appears obvious from the fact that when a certain sense is lacking, there is lacking also the scientific knowledge of things perceived by that sense. A blind man, for instance, cannot have any knowledge of colours. This would not be the case if the soul's intellect were naturally endowed with the concepts of all intelligible objects.

(*S* 1,84,3)[2]

Later, Aquinas praises Aristotle for taking a middle course between the innate idealism of Plato and the crude empiricism of Democritus.

> Aristotle maintained that the intellect had an activity in which the body had no share. Now nothing corporeal can cause an impression on an incorporeal thing, and so, according to Aristotle, the mere stimulus of sensible bodies is not sufficient to cause intellectual activity. Something nobler and higher is needed, which he called the agent intellect: it makes the phantasms received from the senses to be actually intelligible by means of a certain abstraction.
>
> (*S* 1,84,6)[3]

Aquinas contrasts the abstraction made by the intellect with that made by the senses. For even the senses, he explains, do abstract in a way.

> A sense-perceptible form is not in the same manner in the thing outside the soul as it is in the sense-faculty. The sense-faculty receives the forms of sense-perceptible things without their matter, as it receives the colour of gold without the gold; and similarly the intellect receives the ideas of bodies, which are material and changeable, in an immaterial and unchangeable fashion of its own.
>
> (*S* 1,84,1)[4]

The less materially a faculty possesses the form of the object it knows, Aquinas explains, the more perfectly it knows; thus the intellect, which abstracts the ideas not only from matter but also from material individuating characteristics, is a more perfect cognitive power than the senses, which receive the form of what they know without matter but not without material conditions (1,84,2). Perceptible qualities outside the soul are already actually perceptible; but since there are no Platonic Ideas, there is nothing outside the soul actually intelligible corresponding to material objects.

Having rejected Platonic views of the origin of ideas, whether in the pagan form that they derived from self-subsistent forms (*S* 1,84,4) or in the Christian form that they derived from knowledge of the ideas in the mind of God (*S* 1,84,5), Aquinas presents as his own the Aristotelian *via media* between empiricism and Platonism.

> Aristotle took the middle course. He agreed with Plato that the intellect differed from the senses; but he did not accept that the senses had any activity of their own without the participation of the body, so that for him sense-perception was not an activity of the soul alone, but of the soul–body compound. . . . Aristotle agreed with Democritus that the activities of the sense-faculties are caused by the action of empirical objects upon the senses. . . . But he held that the intellect does have an activity in which the body has no share. Now nothing corporeal can have an effect on what is incorporeal. Hence, the cause of intellectual activity must involve more than a mere stimulus from empirical bodies.
>
> (*S* 1,84,6c)[5]

The 'something more' is of course the agent intellect, which we have already encountered, whose function is to make *phantasmata* received from the senses, by abstraction, into actually thinkable objects. Hence sense-perception is not the total and complete cause of intellectual knowledge; it is rather, says Aquinas, 'in some manner the matter of the cause'.

The ideas of the intellect are abstracted, then, from 'phantasms' (*phantasmata*). A visual image, called up when one's eyes are shut; the words one utters to oneself *sotto voce* in the imagination: these are clearly examples of what he means by 'phantasm'. How much else is covered by the word is difficult to determine. Sometimes straightforward cases of seeing events in the world with eyes open seem to be described as a sequence of *phantasmata*: it is not clear whether this means that the word is being used broadly to cover any kind of sense-experience, or whether Aquinas held a regrettable theory that external sense-experience was accompanied by a parallel series of phenomena in the imagination. For our purposes it is not necessary to decide between these alternatives: when Aquinas talks of phantasms we can take him to be speaking of occurrences taking place either in the sense or the imagination. For what he is anxious to elucidate is the role of the intellect within the sensory context provided by the experience of the sentient subject.

Aquinas frequently insists that phantasms play a necessary part not only in the acquisition of concepts, but also in their application.

During our mortal life, he says, 'it is impossible for our intellect to perform any actual exercise of understanding (*aliquid intelligere in actu*) except by attending to phantasms.'

When a concept has been acquired, or when a belief has been formed, the intellect has taken a step from potentiality towards actuality; it is no longer a *tabula rasa*, but has a content; it is in possession of ideas or *species*. But this, according to Aquinas, is not sufficient to enable the intellect to operate unaided: phantasms are needed not only for gaining possession of species but also for making use of them.

Why so? Aquinas puts to himself the following objection:

> It would seem that the intellect can exercise intellectual activity without turning to phantasms, simply by using the species in its possession. For the intellect is placed in a state of actuality by a species informing it. But for the intellect to be in a state of actuality is precisely for it to exercise intellectual activity. Therefore species suffice to enable the intellect to exercise intellectual activity without turning to phantasms.
>
> (*S* 1,84,7 obj. 1)[6]

The answer is to be found by attending to the distinction between two stages of actuality. Possessing a concept or a belief is different from being totally uninformed; but it is different again from exercising the concept or calling the belief to mind. I may know French without, on a given date, speaking, reading or thinking in French; I may believe that the earth is round even when my thoughts are on totally different things. The distinction, in terms of actuality and potentiality, may be made in more than one way. Knowing French is an actuality by comparison with the state of the newborn infant; it is a potentiality by comparison with the activity of actually speaking French. As has been said, the three stages can be distinguished as pure potentiality, first actuality, and second actuality. In these terms, the thesis of 1,84,7 is that phantasms are needed not only to take the intellect from potentiality to first actuality, but also from first actuality to second. Without the jargon, the thesis is that intellectual thought is impossible apart from a sensory context.

Aquinas offers two proofs of this thesis. First, although the intellect has no organ of its own, the exercise of intellect may be impeded by injury to the organs of the imagination (as in a seizure) or of memory (as in a coma). Such brain damage prevents not only the acquisition of new knowledge, but also the utilization of previously acquired knowledge. This shows that the intellectual exercise of habitual knowledge requires the cooperation of imagination and other powers. Second, he says, everyone can experience in his own case that when he tries to understand something, he forms some phantasms for himself by way of examples in which he can so to speak take a look at what he is trying to understand. Similarly 'when we want to make someone understand something, we suggest examples to him from which he can form his own phantasms in order to understand' (1,84,7).

A metaphysical reason is offered to explain this. The proper object of the human intellect in the human body is 'the quiddity or nature existing in corporeal matter'. The quiddities of corporeal things must exist in corporeal individuals.

> Thus, it is part of the concept of a stone that it should be instantiated in a particular stone, and part of the concept of a horse that it should be instantiated in a particular horse, and so on; so the nature of a stone or of any material thing cannot be completely and truly known unless it is known as existing in the particular; but the particular is apprehended by the senses and the imagination. Consequently, in order to have actual understanding of its proper object, the intellect must turn to phantasms to study the universal nature existing in the particular.
>
> (*S* 1a,84,7)[7]

Several things are noteworthy about this whole argument. First, it starts from the premise that there is no bodily organ of the intellect. One might be inclined to ask: how does St Thomas know that brain activity is not necessary for thought, even for the most abstract and intellectual thought? Second, these two possible lines of answers suggest themselves. The first is that St Thomas would agree that there is not in fact, in this life, any thought, however exalted, which is not accompanied by brain activity. But he would say that this was precisely because there was no thought, however exalted, which is not accompanied by the activity of the imagination or senses. The second is that even if brain activity is a necessary condition for thought, this does not make the brain an organ of thought in the way that the eyes are the organ of sight and the tongue and palate are organs of taste. An organ is, as its etymology suggests, something like a tool, a part of the body which can be voluntarily moved and used in characteristic ways which affect the efficiency of the discriminatory activity which it serves. The difficulty is that these two answers seem to cancel out. In the sense of 'organ' in which there is no organ of thought, there is no organ of imagination either – I cannot move my brain in order to imagine better in the way that I can turn my eyes to see better. We may use 'organ' in a broad sense, to mean any part of the body which is intimately related to the exercise of a faculty, so that, in this sense, the visual cortex would be an organ of sight no less than the eye. If so, why should we deny that there is an organ of intellect? Is not the brain just such an organ?

Again, the second argument seems to concern rather the first acquisition of understanding than its later utilization. This is so whether we think of St Thomas as having in mind the production of diagrams (as when in the *Meno* Socrates taught the slave-boy geometry) or the construction of fictional illustrations (as when Wittgenstein imagines primitive language-games in order to throw light on the workings of language). It does not seem to be true that whenever concepts are exercised there must be something going on, even mentally, which is rather like the drawing of a diagram or the telling of a detailed story.

Moreover, the line of argument suggests that the relation of species to phantasm is the same as that of universal to particular. But this is not so, for several reasons. I can have a concept of horse which is not the concept of any particular horse; but equally I can have an image of a horse which is not an image of any particular horse. When I use instances and examples to help grasp a difficult proposition, the instances and examples may be general no less than particular. Thus, suppose I am wondering about the correctness of the logical principle:

If every x has the relation R to some y, then there is some y to which every x has the relation R.

In such a case I will no doubt call up instances and seek for counterexamples. But the propositions I would call to mind – 'every boy loves some girl', 'every road leads to some place' – though less general than the logical principle I am using them to test, are none the less universal and not particular.

Despite all this, it does seem true in one sense that there must be some exercise of sense or imagination, some application to a sensory context, if one is to talk at all of the exercise of concepts or the application of the knowledge of necessary truths. For a man to be exercising the concept, say, of red, it seems that he must be either discriminating red from other colours around him, or having a mental image of redness, or a mental echo of the word 'red', or be talking, reading or writing about redness, or something of the kind. He may indeed be able to *possess* the concept *red* without this showing in his experience or behaviour on a given occasion, but it seems that without some vehicle of sensory activity there could be no *exercise* of the concept on that occasion. Similarly with the knowledge of a general truth, such as that two things that are equal to a third are equal to each other. For this knowledge to be exercised it seems that its possessor must either enunciate it, or apply it, say, in the measurement of objects, or utilise it in some other way even if only in the artful manipulation of symbols.

According to one strand of modern philosophy, thought is essentially operating with symbols; and symbols are signs that bear meaning. Whatever account we are to give of the way in which meaning can be attached to signs, we cannot dispense with the signs to which the meaning is to be attached. The signs may be uttered sounds, or marks on paper: entities perceptible by the senses. Or they may be items in the imagination, such as the words of a fragmentary interior monologue. Either way the signs will provide the sensory context for the intellectual thought.

Every thought is a thought with a content, and a thought with a thinker: it must be somebody's thought, and it must be a thought of something. One may think by talking, whether aloud to others or in silence to oneself. What gives the thought its content, in such a case, is the meaning of the words used; and it is because we grasp that meaning that thinking is an activity of the intellect which is, precisely, the ability to confer and understand meaning. When I think thus, what makes the thought *my* thought is, in the standard spoken case, that it is I who am doing the speaking; in the case of my talking to myself, it is the fact that those images are part of *my* mental history. It is thus that the occurrence of something perceptible by the sense, or something occurring in the imagination, is necessary if I am to have a thought; it is thus that intellectual activity involves *conversio ad phantasmata*.

This seems both true and important, but the nature of Aquinas' arguments for his thesis makes it doubtful whether he understood it in this sense. It is true that it does say that the phantasm employed in the exercise of the concept of A need not be the phantasm of A itself. But when he says this he has in mind particular cases where A is something immaterial and to that extent unpicturable. Whereas it seems that for it to be true that every exercise of a concept involved attention to a phantasm, it would rarely be the case that the phantasm attended to was a representation of the object of the concept. Another difficulty is that Aquinas' mode of argument makes it appear as if the need for thought to take place in a sensory context is a contingent and not a necessary matter, something due to the conditions of our present life. This is something which is not uncongenial to him, since he wishes to defend the possibility of thought in disembodied souls. But if the considerations outlined above are correct, the connection between thought and imagination seems to be a conceptual rather than a contingent matter.

But though Aquinas' arguments seem doubtful, his conclusion seems, as I have already argued, to be correct. Moreover, in answering the third objection to his thesis, he makes a qualification to it which removes the most obvious argument that might be brought against it. The third objection runs thus:

> There are no phantasms of incorporeal things, because the imagination does not go outside the world of time and the continuum. So if our intellect could not operate upon anything without turning to phantasms, it would follow that it could not operate upon anything incorporeal.
>
> $(S$ 1,84,7,3$)^8$

This conclusion would be, of course, quite unacceptable to Aquinas, since he believed that we could have some understanding of God and immaterial angels; and even an atheist has to admit that it is possible to have the thought of an incorporeal deity, though perhaps he may wish to argue that it is an incoherent thought. In reply, Aquinas explains that the understanding of non-bodily entities, though genuine, is limited. Incorporeal substances are known negatively and by analogy.

> Incorporeal things, of which there are no phantasms, are known to us by comparison with empirical bodies of which there are phantasms . . . to understand anything of things of this kind we have to turn to phantasms of empirical bodies, even though there are no phantasms of them.
>
> $(S$ 1,84,7 *ad* 3$)^9$

Aquinas is perhaps too pessimistic about the possibility of there being images of non-bodily things. After all, surely Michelangelo's Sistine Creation *does* contain an image of God. What is true is that the image of a non-bodily thing is not an image of it in virtue of looking like it. However, there is good reason to believe that what makes an image of X an image of X is *never* its resemblance to X, even if X is bodily. (If I paint a picture of Napoleon, it is a picture of Napoleon even if, because I am such a poor painter, it looks more like Nelson.) Be that as it may, Aquinas' answer to his objection does make the valid point that even if it is true that one cannot think of anything without an image, it does not follow that one cannot think of X without an image *of X*. When we think by talking to ourselves, if we talk to ourselves about X, the most common image which will be the vehicle of our thought will not be an image of X (visual, say), but an image (most likely auditory) of the word for X. But of course it may be an image of many other things too, and there are many ways of thinking about X which do not involve talking to ourselves.

8   Universals of thought

In the first article of question eighty-five of the First Part of the *Summa*, St Thomas affirms that the human intellect understands material things by abstracting from phantasms. There appear to be two separable doctrines united in the theory. The first is that concepts and experiences stand in a certain causal relation; the second is that they stand in a certain formal relation.

The causal relation has been spelt out in 1,84,6:

> In this way, then, intellectual activity is caused by the senses of the side of the phantasm. But since phantasms are not sufficient to affect the receptive intellect unless they are made actually intelligible by the agent intellect, sense-knowledge cannot be said to be the total and complete cause of intellectual knowledge, but only the material element of its cause.[1]

To say, then, that concepts are abstracted from experience is to say at least that experience is a necessary causal condition for the acquisition of concepts. How far this is true seems to be partly an empirical matter and partly a philosophical question. It is an empirical matter, for instance, to discover how much a blind man might learn of a textbook on optics. It is a philosophical question how far mastery of such a textbook could count as 'possession of the science of colour' without, for example, the ability to match colours against colour samples.

Besides having a causal relation to experience, Aquinas' ideas have a formal relation to them: that is, concepts on his theory are abstract *in comparison with* experiences. Sense-experience, he believed, is always of a particular individual; intellectual knowledge is primarily of the universal. Consequently, intellectual concepts can be said to abstract from much that is included in sense-experience. This is the sense of 'abstraction' that is suggested in the first article of question eighty-five.

> It is peculiar to the human intellect to know form existing individually in corporeal matter but not *as* existing in such matter. But to know that which is in individual matter but not *as* in such matter is to abstract the form from the individual matter which the phantasms represent.[2]

In answer to an objector, Thomas goes on to clarify:

> What belongs to the specific concept of any material thing such as a stone, or a man, or a horse, can be considered without the individual characteristics which are not part of the specific concept. This is what it is to abstract the universal from the particular, or the intelligible idea from the phantasms, namely to consider the specific nature without considering the individual characteristics which are represented by the phantasm.
>
> (*S* 1,85,1 *ad* 1)[3]

This formal relation is distinct from the causal relation, for what Aquinas says here would be true even if universal concepts were not acquired from experience. Even innate ideas would still be more abstract than representations of individuals, whether these latter were themselves acquired or innate. For to have the concept of man is not to be able to recognize or think of a particular man with particular characteristics. It is, inter alia, to be able to recognize any man no matter what his particular characteristics, to think about men without necessarily attributing particular characteristics to them, and to know general truths about man as such. And this is true no matter how the concept has been acquired.

In modern philosophy there is a familiar, if no longer popular, theory that the acquisition of universal concepts can be explained by selective attention to features of particular experience. One version of the theory was ridiculed long ago by Berkeley in the *Principles of Human Knowledge* (8ff.); more recently Wittgenstein criticized the idea that to understand an ostensive definition means to have in one's mind an idea of the thing defined in the form of a sample or picture.

> So if I am shewn various different leaves and told 'this is called a "leaf" ', I get an idea of the shape of a leaf, a picture of it in my mind. – But what does the picture of a leaf look like when it

does not shew us any particular shape but 'what is common to all shapes of leaf'? Which shade is the 'sample' in my 'mind' of the colour green – the sample of what is common to all shades of green?

(*Philosophical Investigations*, 1,74)

Aquinas' language might make it look as if he held a theory such as Berkeley and Wittgenstein criticized. But in fact this appears unlikely. First of all, the theory described by Wittgenstein demands that an idea be treated quite seriously as a mental *picture*. St Thomas speaks of ideas as being likenesses of the things which are thought of by their aid, and this has sometimes led people to think that he was talking of mental images. But according to his terminology mental images seem rather to be phantasms, and phantasms are sharply distinguished from ideas. Phantasms, he says, come and go from day to day, but ideas remain for life; the image of one man differs from the image of another, but both are recognized as men by one and the same idea or *species*.

Indeed, Aquinas expressly rejects the idea that a concept is just a mental image shorn of inessential features:

Through the power of the agent intellect and through its attention (*conversio*) to the phantasms, there results in the receptive intellect a certain likeness which is a representation of the things whose phantasms they are, but only in respect of their specific nature. It is thus that the intelligible concept is said to be abstracted from the phantasms; it is not that numerically the same form, which was at one time in the phantasms, later comes into the receptive intellect, in the way in which a body may be taken from one place and transferred to another.

(*S* 1,85,1)[4]

Aquinas is aware that the charge can be made that on his account the intellect distorts reality in the very process of grasping it. He puts to himself the following objection:

A thought which thinks a thing otherwise than it is is a false thought. But the forms of material things are not abstracted from the particulars represented in experience. Hence, if we think of material things by abstracting ideas from experience, there will be falsehood in our thought.

(*S* 1,85,1)[5]

His reply depends upon distinguishing two senses of the ambiguous sentence 'A thought which thinks a thing otherwise than it is is a false thought.' To think a thing *to be* otherwise than it is is certainly to think falsely. But if all that is meant by our 'thinking a thing otherwise than it is' is that the way it is with our thinking when we think is different from the way it is with the thing we are thinking about, in its own existence, then there need be no false-hood involved. To think that Julius Caesar had no weight would be to think a false thought; but there is no falsehood involved in thinking of Julius Caesar without thinking of his weight, though Julius Caesar himself could not exist without his weight. Similarly, Aquinas argued, there can be, without any distortion or falsehood, a thought of human nature which does not contain a thought of any individual matter, though there never was an instance of human nature without any individual matter (*S* 1,85,1 *ad* 1).

Is Aquinas an idealist? Does he believe that we never really know or understand the world itself, but only immaterial and abstract ideas?

The answer to this question is complicated. In Aquinas' system there seem to be decriptions of two different types of ideas: ideas that are mental abilities, and ideas that are mental objects.

Sometimes we read of ideas that are dispositions or modifi-cations of the intellect. Ideas of things in this sense seem to be what would nowadays be called 'concepts': you have a concept of X, for instance, if you have mastered the use of a word for X in some language. Ideas may be ideas *that*, instead of being ideas *of*: an idea *that* such and such is the case would be an instance of an idea corresponding to Aquinas' second type of acts of the intellect, just as an idea *of* something corresponds to the first type of act. An idea *that*, considered as a disposition, would be a belief or opinion or something of the kind, rather than a simple concept. In this sense, then, ideas are dispositions corresponding to the two types of thought which are the activities by which the intellect is defined.

If a philosopher thinks of ideas in this way, he is unlikely to be tempted to think of ideas as the *objects* of our understanding, as *what* we know when we have knowledge. If I am thinking about the North Pole, no doubt I am making use of, employing, or exercising my concept of the North Pole; but my concept is not what I am thinking *about*. If I think that the North Pole is a cold sort of place, or that it was discovered by Peary, I am not thinking that my concept is cold or was discovered by Peary, but that the Pole itself is/was. Of course I *can* think about my concept of the

North Pole: I can reflect, for instance, that it is a rather thin, hazy and childish one; but in thinking that thought in turn I am not thinking that the North Pole is thin, hazy and childish; and I am exercising not merely my concept of the North Pole, but also my concept of *concept*. When we take ideas in this sense, then, it may be true to say that all thought uses ideas, but it is obviously untrue to say that all thought is about ideas.

Aquinas makes this point quite clearly:

> Some thinkers have maintained that our cognitive powers are aware only of their own modifications . . . thus the intellect would think of nothing but its own modifications, that is the ideas which it takes in. On this view, ideas of this kind are the very object of thought.
>
> But this opinion is obviously false. . . . If the only objects of thought were ideas in our souls, it would follow that all the sciences are not about things outside the soul but only about ideas in the soul.
>
> (*S* 1,85,2)[6]

The truth is that ideas are not *what* is thought of, but that by which thought takes place:

> But because the intellect reflects on itself, by the same act of reflection it thinks of its own thinking and of the idea by which it thinks. And thus the idea is a secondary object of thought; but the primary object of thought is the thing of which the idea is a likeness.
>
> (*S* 1,85,2)[7]

Aquinas, then, explicitly rejects the idealist doctrine that the mind can think of nothing but its own ideas. But there are a number of features of his writing which tempt the reader to think that he regarded ideas not simply as abilities or dispositions to think in certain ways, but as the primary objects of thought. In the passage quoted above, as in many other places, Aquinas speaks of the idea as a likeness of the thing of which it is an idea; and this suggests that ideas are pictures or images from which we read off the features of their originals. If this were right, then external things would be the primary objects of thought only in the sense in which, when I look at myself in the mirror, I 'see' myself rather than seeing the mirror, unless I am making an especial effort to attend to the mirror. But this would be a wrong way to interpret Aquinas:

elsewhere he expressly distinguishes between mental images in the imagination (*idola* or *phantasmata*) and the ideas of the intellect; and in explaining what he means by saying that an idea is a likeness of its object, the comparison he introduces is not that of portrait to original, but that of the resemblance between cause and effect in natural processes.

There are two kinds of actions, Aquinas says: those which result in changes in the patient on which the agent acts, and those which affect nothing but the agent. Sometimes he calls actions of the first kind 'transient' and actions of the second kind 'immanent'. When a fire heats a kettle, we have an action of the first kind, and when I think of a kettle, we have an action of the second kind. Heating the kettle brings about a change in the kettle, but thinking of the kettle, of itself, affects nothing but the thinker. What heats the kettle is the heat of the fire; when the kettle is heated, it becomes hot, like the fire: the cause of the heating resembles the object after the change. St Thomas goes on:

> Similarly, the form operative in an immanent action is a like-ness of the object. Thus, the likeness of a visible thing is operative in the sight of vision, and the likeness of an object of thought, i.e. an idea, is operative in the thinking of the intellect.
> (*S*,85,2)[8]

The parallel seems clumsily drawn: the way in which the terminus of an immanent action (a particular thought) resembles the operat-ive form (an idea or concept) is that both of them are *of the same object*; but it is their similarity to each other, not to the object *of* which they are, that is parallel to the heating of the kettle.

Is there, then, any sense in which an idea or thought is like its object? Surely nothing could be more different than say, salt and my being able to recognize salt: indeed, 'difference' seems too weak a word to describe the gulf between the two items. But an idea is like its object in this way: in order to identify an idea one has to describe its content; and the description of the content of the idea is the very same as the description of the idea's object. For instance, the idea that the world will shortly come to an end might be said to be the idea of a certain state of affairs. To specify *which* idea is involved, and to specify *which* state of affairs is involved one uses exactly the same expression 'that the world will shortly come to an end'.

Earlier, we considered Aquinas' thesis that the operation of a sense-faculty was identical with the action of a sense-object: for instance, my tasting the sweetness of the sugar was the same as the sugar's tasting sweet to me. It is now time to consider the analogous theorem about the intellect: thought in operation is identical with the object of thought (*intelligibile in actu est intellectus in actu*) (*S* 1,14,2; 55,1 *ad* 2).

Unlike some other scholars, I believe that the identity between the object of thought in act and the intellect itself in operation is intended by Aquinas as no less real an identity than the corresponding identity in the case of sense-perception. Aquinas' theory of intentionality can be summed up thus: the object of thought exists, intentionally, in the intellect; its existence is the actualization, the life, of the intellect.

We must remember that intentional existence and immaterial existence are not the same thing. A pattern exists, naturally and materially, in a coloured object; it exists, intentionally and materially, in the eye, or, according to Aquinas, in the lucid medium. The Archangel Gabriel is a form which exists immaterially and naturally in its own right; it exists immaterially and intentionally in Raphael's thought of Gabriel. The characteristic of intellectual thought, whether of men or of angels, is that it is the existence of a form in a mode which is both intentional and immaterial.

Aquinas, I have said, is committed to the identity of the objects of thought and the activity of the thinker just as he is to the identity of the activity of a sense-object and the activity of the sense-faculty. But there is no doubt that the doctrine about thought is more difficult to understand than the doctrine about sense-perception. However, it applies, I believe, to all objects of thought, whereas in considering the theorem about sense-perception we were forced to restrict its application to the comparatively narrow range of the 'proper sensibles'. Most properties perceptible by the senses, I have argued, have other exercises besides the exercise of bringing the senses into operation.

It is different with the corresponding intellectual theorem: *intellectus in actu est intelligibile in actu*. The actuality of the power of the object of thought is the same thing as the actuality of the power of thinking. That is to say, on the one hand the intellect just is the capacity for intellectual thought, the locus of thought; the intellect has no structure or matter; it is just the capacity for thought. On the other hand, the object of intellectual thought, a universal as such, is something which has no existence outside thought.

We can now sum up in answer to the question: 'Does thought resemble its objects?' If we are thinking of the universal objects of thought, then 'resemblance' is too weak a word to describe the closeness between thought and object. The relationship between the two is not one of resemblance but of identity – identity in actuality. If we are thinking, however, of the material objects in the world, then the resemblance is one of similarity, as described above: the object and the thought resemble each other in that they are both informed by the same form; they differ from each other because the mode of existence of the form is totally different in the two cases.

According to the thesis defended in article seven of question eighty-four, which we saw in the previous chapter, imagery, or a sensory context, is necessary for thought of any kind, including the most abstract, metaphysical, or theological thought. But when we turn to consider thought about concrete individuals – the kind of thought expressed by a proposition such as 'Socrates is mortal' – then the senses and the imagination are involved in an even more intimate way. This is spelt out in two stages. In article three of question eighty-five Aquinas asks whether our intellect knows what is more universal before it knows what is less universal; in article one of question eighty-six he asks whether our intellect knows individuals.

The theses which set the problem are boldly stated in the discussion, in 1,85,3, of whether intellectual knowledge of the more universal is prior to intellectual knowledge of the less universal. The first thing to be said on this topic, according to Aquinas, is this:

> Intellectual knowledge in a certain manner takes its origin from sense knowledge. And since the object of the sense is the singular, and the object of the intellect is the universal, it must be the case that the knowledge of singulars, in our case, is prior to the knowledge of universals.
>
> $(S\ 1,85,3)^9$

We know the singular before the universal (for instance, when we are babies innocent of language); but our *intellect* can be said baldly to have as its object the universal alone. This seems correct. A child sees dogs long before it acquires the concept 'dog'; seeing is of the individual, because one cannot see a dog that is not any particular dog; the concept is of the universal, because there is no theoretical limit on the number of things which may fall under the description 'dog'.

But in the case both of the senses and of the intellect, Aquinas says, more general precedes less general knowledge. From a distance you can tell that something is a tree before you can tell that it is a beech; you can spot a dog without being able to decide whether it is a labrador or an alsatian; you can see a human being coming before you recognize the person as male or female, John or Mary. Here Aquinas appeals to the authority of Aristotle:

> Thus, at the beginning, a child distinguishes man from not-man before distinguishing one man from another; that is why, as Aristotle says, a child begins by calling all men 'father' and only later distinguishes between each of them.
>
> $(S\ 1,85,3)^{10}$

The illustration is not really very helpful, because one wants to know how Aristotle decides whether the child (a) means 'man' by 'father' or (b) means 'father' but believes that everyone he sees is his father.

The fact seems to be that in the case of a faculty such as a sense, which is a faculty for discrimination, the precise discrimination is, logically, subsequent to the imprecise discrimination; progress in discrimination is progress from the less determinate to the more determinate. But in the case of the intellect it seems we cannot make the same generalization. Sometimes we proceed from the more general to the less general, and sometimes in the opposite direction. We may acquire the concept 'tree' before learning the different kinds of tree; on the other hand, a child may have mastered 'dog' and 'cat' before she has the more general term 'animal', and in adult life it may take a degree of sophistication to regard both heat and light as species of a common genus.

Both genus and species are related as more general and less general within the realm of the universal; but according to Aquinas' regular teaching the relation between species and individual is quite different from that between genus and species. There is one surprising passage in article four of question eighty-five where it almost seems as if Aquinas had forgotten this. He says:

> If we consider the nature of genus and species as it is in individuals, we find that it stands in the relation of formal

principle with respect to individuals; for the individual is individual because of its matter, but it belongs to a species by virtue of its form. But the nature of the genus is related to the nature of the species in the manner of a material principle; because the nature of the genus is taken from what is material in a thing, but the specific element from what is formal; as animality is derived from the sensory part, and humanity from the intellectual part.
(1,85,4)[11]

At first sight, this looks as if Aquinas is suggesting that genus is related to species as species is related to individual. This would be quite wrong, on his own principles; the two relationships cannot be treated as parallel instances of the relation of indeterminate to determinate. Genus is indeed related to species as indeterminate to determinate, but species is not related to individual as indeterminate to determinate. No collection of determinations will individuate a particular individual.

But Aquinas is not saying that the individual is related to the species as determinate to indeterminate. He is saying that in a given individual the matter can be regarded, like genus, as something indeterminate. Just as there is no animal that is not a particular kind of animal – no animal which belongs to the genus but to no species of the genus – so too there is no matter which is not matter of a particular kind, matter informed by a specific form. But it would be wrong to say that matter is to form as indeterminate to determinate; the truth is that matter is to informed matter as indeterminate to determinate.

9   Knowledge of particulars

Aquinas has a special problem in giving an account of intellectual knowledge of individuals because of his thesis that individuation is by matter. Some philosophers have thought that an object could be individuated by listing the totality of its properties. Since to have a property is to fall under some universal – to be square, for example, is to be an instance of the universal 'square' – if an item can be individuated by its properties, all we need to identify an individual is to list the universals under which it falls. But Aquinas rightly rejected this: in theory, however long a list of universals we draw up, it is always logically possible that more than one individual will answer to the list.

One of Aquinas' clearest statements on this topic occurs in the second question of *De Veritate*, in article five, where the topic is God's knowledge of singulars. According to Avicenna, Aquinas says, God knows each singular in a universal manner, by knowing all the universal causes which produce singulars.

> Thus, if an astronomer knew all the motions of the heavens and the distances between all the heavenly bodies, he would know every eclipse which is to occur within the next hundred years; but he would not know any of them as a particular individual, in such a way as to know whether or not it was now occurring, in the way that a peasant knows that while he is seeing it. And it is in this manner that they maintain that God knows singulars; not as if he intuited the singular nature of them, but by positing the universal causes.

But this account, Aquinas maintains, is quite inadequate, for the following reason:

From universal causes nothing follows except universal forms, unless there is something to individuate the forms. But however many universal forms you pile up, you never make them add up to anything singular. For it always remains possible to think of that totality of forms being instantiated more than once.

(*V* 5,2)[1]

All this is well and clearly said, and it underlines Aquinas' problem. If the intellect – human no less than divine – is a faculty for grasping universals, how can there be intellectual knowledge of a singular individual?

It is in the brief article one of question eighty-six that Aquinas finally gives his answer to the question whether our intellect knows individuals. 'Directly and primarily', he says, 'our intellect cannot know individuals among material things.'

The reason is that the principle of individuation in material things is individual matter, and our intellect, as said before, operates by abstracting intelligible species from that kind of matter. But what is abstracted from individual matter is universal. Therefore our intellect has direct knowledge only of universals.

(1,86,1c)[2]

There was a time when I found this thesis shocking and incredible. Shocking, because if it is impossible to have intellectual knowledge of an individual, it must be equally impossible to have spiritual love for an individual; for the will can relate only to what the intellect can grasp. Hence love between human individuals must be mere sensuality. Incredible, because one of the time-honoured paradigms of intellectual activity is the formulation of syllogisms such as 'All men are mortal; Socrates is a man; therefore Socrates is mortal.' But one cannot formulate singular propositions, in a real case, if one cannot understand what is meant by the individual terms which occur in them. How much preferable to Aquinas' teaching, I used to think, is the belief in the Scotist tradition that each individual has a *haecceitas*, a unique essence, which can be grasped as such by the intellect!

Later, however, I have come to see that Aquinas was right to maintain that our knowledge of material individuals cannot be something which is purely intellectual. This can be made clear if we reflect that the intellect is, above all, the human capacity to master language and to think those thoughts which are expressible only in language. There is no way in which we can uniquely identify an individual in language without going outside language itself and latching on to the context within which the language is used.

Let us apply the considerations which Aquinas used about the knowledge of an individual eclipse to the knowledge of an individual human being. When I think of a particular person there will be, if I know her well, many descriptions I can give in language to identify who I mean. But unless I bring in reference to particular times and places there may be no description I can give which would not in theory be satisfiable by a human being other than the one I mean. As Aquinas emphasized, I cannot individuate simply by enumerating a list of attributes. Only perhaps by pointing, or taking you to see her, can I settle beyond doubt which person I mean; and pointing and vision go beyond pure intellectual thought.

Similarly, if I bring in spatio-temporal individuating references, I have left the realm of intellectual thought; from the point of view of a pure spirit there would be no such framework. It is only by linking universal intellectual ideas with sensory experience that we know individuals and are capable of forming singular propositions. And that is what Aquinas says.

> Indirectly, and by a certain kind of reflection, the intellect can know an individual; because, as said above, even after it has abstracted species it cannot make use of them in intellectual operation unless it turns towards the phantasms in which it grasps the intelligible species, as Aristotle says. Thus, what the intellect grasps directly by the intelligible species is the universal; but indirectly it grasps individuals which have phantasms. And that is how it forms the proposition 'Socrates is a man.'
>
> $(S\ 1,86,1c)$[3]

Let us contrast this position of Aquinas with corresponding positions in Duns Scotus. For Scotus there exists an individual essence for each substance which is an object of knowledge: the *haecceitas* of Scotist tradition. The *haecceitas* is a form, and therefore it can be present in the intellect. Because each thing has within it a formal, intelligible principle, the ground is cut beneath the basis on which Aquinas rested the need for a species-specific *intellectus agens* in human beings.

Individuals, unlike universals, are things which come into and go out of existence. If the proper objects of the intellect include not only universals but individuals – even individual forms like a *haecceitas* – then there is a possibility of such an object being in the intellect and not existing in reality – one and the same object being in the intellect and not existing in reality – a possibility which Aquinas' theory was careful to avoid. An individual form may exist in the mind and yet the corresponding individual not exist. Hence the individual form present in the intellect can be only a representation of, and not identical with, that whose knowledge it embodies. Hence, a window is opened, at the level of the highest intellectual knowledge, a window to permit the entry of the epistemological problems which have been familiar to us since Descartes.

In Aquinas' account no such window exists, because there is nothing in the mind which the mind has not itself created. Of course, like all philosophers, Aquinas has to deal with problems of error in sense-perception, but the way in which this problem presents itself to him is a question of describing and accounting for the malfunctioning of a faculty (*S* 1,17,2). It is not a question of building a bridge between a correctly functioning faculty, or a correctly functioning cognitive apparatus, and an extra-mental reality. But that is what, through Scotus and often in Descartes, the epistemological problem more and more explicitly became.

After treating of the knowledge of individuals, the remainder of question eighty-six is devoted to exploring the extent of human intellectual activity. Is the capacity of our intellect infinite? If not, what limits are set to its powers? Can it know what is contingent? Can it know what is future?

Several reasons are offered, in article two, for believing that the intellect can know an infinite number of things. The intellect can know God, the supreme infinite; it can grasp the number series, which is endless. There could not be an infinite number of bodies in a single place, because bodies take up space; but ideas do not get in each others' way, so there is no reason why there should not, dispositionally, be an infinite number of them in a single mind.

In reply Aquinas makes a distinction between potential, actual and dispositional knowledge; and he reminds us that the object of the intellect is the quiddity of material things.

In material things there is no actual infinity, but only potential infinity, in the unending succession of one thing after another. Hence, in our intellect, there is a potential infinity, in grasping one thing after another. There never comes a point where our intellect has grasped so much that it cannot grasp anything more.

$$(S\ 1,86,2)^4$$

We cannot, however, have a simultaneous grasp of an infinite number of things; this would be impossible by definition, because infinity, according to Aristotle in the *Physics* (207a7), is a quantity such that however much you take of it, there is always something over.

So far, what Aquinas has said is easy to accept. But why should he go on to deny that we have a dispositional (*habitualis*) knowledge of infinity? Is not that exactly what a mastery of the natural number series is? Aquinas denies the possibility on the grounds that dispositional knowledge must be subsequent to actual thinking about what is known, as if one could only know the natural number series if one had counted in one's head to infinity. But surely, part of what it is to master the series of natural numbers is to know that however far you have counted, you could always count further if you wanted to. Aquinas says that knowing the rule which generates a series is only knowing the terms of the series 'indistinctly and potentially'; but in fact it is a more genuine intellectual knowledge of the terms than would be given by a series of mental images of individual terms in succession, which is what Aquinas offers as the alternative account of mathematical knowledge (*S* 1,86,3 *ad* 2).

Our knowledge of God, he says, is not such as to constitute knowledge of the infinite; in this life we know Him only through His limited, material effects, and even in the afterlife we will not be able to comprehend Him in His totality. And our ideas, Aquinas claims, *do* get in each other's way; we can only think of one thing at a time, and ideas have to come into our minds one after another. But this seems to show at most that we cannot think of two things at once; it does not seem to rule out the possibility of an unlimited number of ideas as dispositions, though of course in a finite life not all of these can be brought into the forefront of the mind. But perhaps it is futile to argue whether our knowledge of the number series is to be regarded as one idea of an infinite series, or as an infinite number of ideas of individual terms.

Aquinas' treatment of the intellect's knowledge of the contingent is brief and crisp, and the body of the article deserves to be quoted in full:

Contingent things can be considered in two ways: first, precisely as contingent; second, as containing an element of necessity – for nothing is so contingent as to exclude all necessity. It is a contingent fact that Socrates is running; but the relation between running and moving is a necessary one; for it is a necessary truth that if Socrates is running, he is moving.

Contingency in things arises from matter. What is contingent is what can be or not be, and that potentiality is something which belongs to matter. Necessity, on the other hand, is a consequence of the nature of form; for properties which are entailed by a form are necessary properties. But matter is the principle of individuation, because universality is a consequence of the abstraction of a form from particular matter. As has been said, it is universals which are the direct and essential object of the intellect; individuals are the object of the senses and only indirectly of the intellect.

Thus contingent things, as contingent, are known directly by the senses and only indirectly by the intellect; but the universal and necessary aspects of contingent things are known by the intellect.

All science, then, is concerned with the necessary and universal aspects of their objects; but the subject-matter of particular sciences may be either necessary or contingent.

(*S* 1,86,3)[5]

As examples of sciences which deal with the contingent Aquinas mentions moral sciences, which deal with human actions subject to free will, and physical sciences which deal with bodies which come into and pass out of existence.

From what has been said about knowledge of the contingent, it is clear what is to be said about knowledge of the future. Future events are temporal individuals of which the human intellect can have no direct knowledge; but it can know universal and necessary truths which apply to future as well as to past and present. Moreover, we can know the future in so far as it is contained in present causes: with certainty if the causes are necessitating causes (as when the astronomer predicts an eclipse), or with varying degrees of probability where our knowledge is based on tendencies which fall short of necessitation (as in our conjectures about human affairs) (*S* 1,86,4).

10 Self-knowledge

We come, then, finally to the question how, within this theoretical framework, to account for knowledge of the individual self. The question of self-knowledge can be put in more than one way. We may ask: how does a human individual know himself? Or we may ask: how does the human intellect know itself? Aquinas prefers, in question eighty-seven, the second formulation. This is perhaps surprising in view of his correct insistence elsewhere that it is a human being who thinks and understands, just as it is a human being (and not, say, an eye) which sees. Equally surprisingly, the first question which he puts to himself, in connection with the intellect's self-knowledge, is whether the intellect knows itself by its essence. We may well wonder whether talk of the essence of an individual intellect does not, in the end, involve Aquinas in believing in something very like a Scotist *haecceitas*.

Let us postpone, for the moment, the question of the essence of the individual intellect, and consider what St Thomas thought about the essence of an individual human being. One might first try to distinguish a Thomist individual essence from a Scotist *haecceitas* by saying that it includes matter. But according to St Thomas the essence of a human being does not include any individual matter (*materia signata*);it does not include any particular parcel of matter, but only some matter or other. The essence of a human being is what makes him a human being, which includes having a body; but the essence does not include having *this* body, or a body composed of *this* matter. For St Thomas as for Scotus there are individual essences; but whereas for Scotists it is the *haecceitas* which individuates, for the Thomist it is the other way round: the essence is individuated by its possessor. My soul, my essence, my intellect are the soul, essence, intellect they are, are the individual items they are, because they are the soul of Anthony Kenny, who is *this* body. Even if, as Aquinas thought, they can survive my death, they are still the individuals they are because they belonged to this *body*.

If we bear this in mind, we realize that my soul does not have an essence except in the sense that it is the spiritual aspect of *my* essence. If Aquinas puts the question whether the intellect knows itself by its own essence, that is not because he believes that it has an independent essence, but because that was what was believed by those Platonists whose view he is attacking here. If the human intellect were a pure spirit in contact with some world of pure Ideas, then its self-knowledge too would no doubt be some spiritual self-translucence. But *our* minds are not like that, at least in the present life.

> Our intellect becomes the object of its own intellectual activity in so far as it is actualized by species abstracted from empirical things by the light of the active intellect . . . . So it is not by any essence of itself, but through its activity that our intellect knows itself.
>
> (*S* 1,87,1)[1]

But intellectual self-knowledge is of two very different kinds. There is first of all the self-knowledge of the individual: Socrates perceives that he has an intellectual soul by perceiving his own intellectual activity. But there is also the human race's knowledge of what human understanding is: this is something gathered painfully by philosophical toil, and many human beings never rightly acquire it. The first kind of knowledge, Aquinas says, presents no such problem.

> In order to have the first kind of knowledge of the mind, the mind's own presence is sufficient, since it is the principle of the act by which the mind perceives itself.
>
> (*S* 1,87,1)[2]

This deceptively simple statement needs careful elucidation, which is offered in the second and third articles of question eighty-seven. Aquinas' guiding principle is this: 'nothing is known except so far as it is actual' (*nihil cognoscitur nisi secundum quod est actu*). One application of this principle is that it is by seeing what people do that you discover what they can do. To find out whether someone can speak French, or perform long division, the best way is to get them actually to speak French or actually to do the sum. But there are, as we have seen before, degrees of actuality: speaking French is an actuality by comparison with knowing French, but knowing French is an actuality by comparison with being able to learn French. In each case, we discover the truth about what is less actual by investigating what is more actual: thus, we can find out whether a dog has learned to retrieve by seeing whether he actually does retrieve; and we discover whether cats have the capacity to learn to retrieve by seeing whether they actually can be taught.

So, too, the essence of the human intellect is to be understood by investigating the powers of the human intellect (for example, the ability to learn language), the powers of the human intellect have to be understood by investigating the dispositions of the human intellect (for example, knowledge of English) and the dispositions of the human intellect have to be understood by investigating the activities of the human intellect (for example, the actual use of language).

Thus, in article two Aquinas says that a person perceives he has a disposition (or *habitus*) by perceiving that he exhibits the activity appropriate to it. (For instance, I can check that I still know 'The Charge of the Light Brigade' by reciting it.) This kind of knowledge, he says, is produced simply by the presence of the disposition; because it is by its presence that it causes the activity by which it is immediately perceived.

Thus it is the intellect's knowledge of its own acts which is prior to its knowledge of its dispositions or its powers or its essence: the basis of all self-knowledge is the fact that when we think, we know that we are thinking. But there is no such thing as pure thinking: whenever we think, we are thinking of something, or thinking that something. Hence the very first step towards self-knowledge is the knowledge *what* we are thinking, our knowledge of the object of thought. (I could not know that I was engaged in proving Pythagoras' theorem if I did not know what that theorem itself was.) The primary object of human thought, as Aquinas insists again and again, is the nature of material things. Thus Aquinas sums up:

What is first known by the human intellect is this object; then, in the second place, the activity by which the object known is itself known; and finally, by way of this activity, the intellect itself is known, through the thinking which is the intellect's function.

$$(S \; 1,87,3c)^3$$

If the basis of self-knowledge is the intellect's awareness of its own activities, are we not in danger of an infinite regress? For if whenever I think I think that I think, then whenever I think that I think I must think that I think that I think, and so on (S 1,87,3,2). Aquinas' reply to this objection is not altogether clear. He says that my knowing the nature, say, of gold is not the same as knowing that I know the nature of gold. But that does not seem to stop the regress. Perhaps he regards it as producing only a harmless potential infinity. At all events, it seems to be the case that if I am justified in saying that I know that p, then I am justified in saying that I know that I know that p and so on.

The difficulty in Aquinas' account arises rather in his claim that the intellect 'perceives' its activities, and that it is from this perception that all self-knowledge arises.   We may wonder whether on Aquinas' own principles matters ought to be as simple as this. The intellect is a faculty for the grasping of universals: what is this 'perceiving' that we are now told is one of its activities? If it is a perceiving involving knowledge of an individual – whether the mind itself or one of its individual acts – it seems that it must operate indirectly, through reflection on phantasms. But we are given no account of how reflection on phantasms helps the mind to knowledge of that individual which is itself. Aquinas has explained that what makes a thought the thought of an individual object is its relation to phantasms which are related to that object. But what makes the thought the thought of an individual *subject*: i.e. what makes my thoughts *my* thoughts?

This question arises about general thoughts as well as thoughts about individuals. Consider mathematical thoughts. Innumerable people besides myself believe that two and two make four. When I believe this, what makes the belief *my* belief? What of the belief that I am Anthony Kenny? Surely *that* thought, at least, individuates its thinker. Well, the thought 'I am Napoleon' can be thought truly only by Napoleon, but the very same thought may be thought, falsely, by someone other than Napoleon, suffering from a delusion. There is nothing in the content of a thought which makes it one person's thought rather than another.

The question may seem a bizarre one, but it is not one which it is inappropriate to put to Aquinas. In his time it was the subject of lively controversy between Latin and Arabic interpreters of Aristotle. Aquinas insisted, against the Averroists, that a thought such as I have mentioned is my thought, and not the thought of any world-soul, or supra-individual agent intellect. In his *De Unitate Intellectus* he sets out to demolish the Averroist account of human thought.

Averroes, Aquinas says, held the receptive intellect to be a substance quite separate from any human being; an intelligible species was the form and act of this intellect, but it had two subjects, or possessors, namely the receptive intellect and the phantasm of an individual human. Thus, the receptive intellect is linked to us by its form by means of the phantasms; so that when the receptive intellect understands, an individual human being understands. But this account, says Aquinas, is empty (*U* 63–4).

Of the three reasons which Aquinas gives to prove the futility of the Averroist position, the following is the most persuasive. It is true, Aquinas says, that one item may have more than one subject or possessor. A wall's looking red to me may be the very same event as my seeing the redness of the wall. The same event is thus, as it were, an item in my history and an item in the history of the wall. So there is no objection in principle to the idea that a species may be both a form of the receptive intellect and something which belongs to the phantasms. But that would not make the human being, whose phantasms these are, be an intelligent subject.

> The link between the receptive intellect and the human being, who is the possessor of the phantasms whose species are in the receptive intellect, is the same as the link between the coloured wall and the faculty of sight which has an impression of that colour. But the wall does not see, but is seen; it would follow therefore that the human being is not the thinker, but that its phantasms are thought of by the receptive intellect.
>
> (*U* 65)[4]

The answer to the question what makes my thoughts mine cannot, then, be that their intellectual content is embodied in mental images which are the products of my body. Instead, Aquinas says, the thoughts I think are *my* thoughts because the soul which thinks them is the form of *my* body.

But is Aquinas' own answer in the end very different from the

Averroist one he rejects? He maintains that the soul can exist, and think, without the body. But, given the general Aristotelian hylomorphic theory to which he is committed, if X is the form of Y, then operations of X are operations of Y. Of course Aquinas denied that thinking is the operation of any bodily organ, and in that he is correct, if we are using 'organ' in the sense in which the eye is the organ of sight. But though thinking is not the operation of any bodily organ, it is the activity of a body, namely the thinking human being. That is to say, the manifestations, expressions, of my thoughts are the movements of my body, just as in general the manifestation of my knowledge of a language such as English consists in the movements of my speaking lips, my reading eyes, my writing fingers, my acting limbs. Hence it is not enough to say that my thoughts are *my* thoughts because the soul which thinks them is the form of my body: it is necessary to spell out the way in which my body expresses the thoughts if the thoughts expressed are to be my thoughts.

But are there not unexpressed thoughts, the thoughts which pass through our minds in private, unvoiced, thinking? Indeed there are, and we may well ask: what is it that makes these thoughts my thoughts? It may seem unhelpful, though it is true, to reply: they are thoughts which, if they were expressed, would be expressed by me. To make this answer seem less vacuous, and to convince ourselves that even in this case the criterion for the possessor is still bodily, we should reflect on cases of alleged telepathy or thought-reading. This is not meant to endorse the hypothesis that there are genuine such phenomena; it is meant to be a concession for the sake of argument to those who want to take a highly spiritualist view of the mind. Even in such a case, I will show, the criterion for the possessor of the thought is bodily and not spiritual.

Suppose that at a thought-reading session, or seance, the thought-reader or medium says 'Someone in this room is thinking of Eustace'. Here, ex hypothesi, the occurrence of the thought has been ascertained by means other than normal bodily communication. Even here, the way we would seek to decide whether what the thought-reader claimed was true would involve appeal to bodily criteria. What settles the matter is whose hand goes up, whose voice confesses to the private thought. And *whose* the hand is, *whose* the voice is, is determined by looking to see whose body is involved.

Let there be no misunderstanding here. It is not being suggested that it is by observing actual or conjecturing hypothetical movements of my own body that I decide which thoughts are my own thoughts. Aquinas is indeed right that we 'perceive', that is to say, know without any intermediary, what we are thinking. The question 'Are these thoughts my thoughts?' is not one which is always absurd: one might put the question, perhaps in disgust, in reading vapid outpourings in a long-lost adolescent diary found when cleaning out a cupboard. But there is no state of mind in which I know that certain thoughts are currently being thought, and wonder whose thoughts there are, mine or someone else's. It is not by bodily criteria that I know which thoughts are mine, or know what I am thinking, because it is not by any criteria at all that I know these matters. But what it is that I know, when I know that certain thoughts are mine, is the same thing that other people know when they know what I am thinking; and what I know, and what they know, are something to which the bodily criteria are necessarily relevant.

Let us sum up, then, the residual, unresolved, difficulty which vitiates Aquinas' account of self-knowledge. It is correct, as Aquinas often says (for example, at *S* 1,75,6), that my thoughts are my thoughts because they are operations of the form of my body. But the only account which he gives of the way in which my body is involved in the operation of the intellect is his account of the way in which the phantasms are involved in our present life, at every level, in the exercise of thought. It is only by reifying the intellect, by treating form as something separable from matter, that he is able to avoid the Averroist account of the relation between intellect and imagination which, as he rightly says, is empty.

Question eighty-seven, on self-knowledge, is the last question of the *Summa* which a philosophical student of Aquinas' psychology needs to study in detail. The remaining questions take us into areas dominated by Aquinas' theological presuppositions. Thus, the opening of question eighty-eight is not such as to whet the appetite of a modern reader. The question is devoted to the way in which the human soul knows immaterial substances; and the first issue raised is 'whether the human soul, in this life, is able to understand, in themselves, the immaterial substances we call angels'. Few nowadays, even among orthodox Christians, appear to believe in the literal existence of spiritual creatures of a superhuman kind; and it may seem of little interest to ask how human beings could come to the knowledge of such beings if there were any.

In fact, as we read through the text, we discover that the direction of the argument is itself highly agnostic. St Thomas did indeed believe in angels, on the basis of various biblical passages; but in this question his only invocation of Scripture is to cite Wisdom 9,16 ('Who can discover what is in the heavens?') in support of the conclusion that angels cannot be known by human inquiry. The purpose of the three articles of the question is to reject the attempts of various philosophers to attribute to the embodied human soul something which might be called 'knowledge of immaterial substances'.

By 'immaterial substance' a philosopher may try to mean items of very different kinds. In this question St Thomas considers four kinds of alleged immaterial substances: the Platonic Ideas, the subsistent Agent Intellect of Arabian Aristotelians, the human soul, and God. The angels of Christian tradition, after the title, are hardly mentioned.

In each case St Thomas denies, or strictly limits, the possibility of intellectual understanding of immaterial substance. There are no Platonic Ideas, and the Agent Intellect is not an immaterial substance but a faculty of the human soul. The only knowledge which the embodied soul can have of any immaterial substances there may be is knowledge derived from its own knowledge of itself; and its knowledge of itself is knowledge of a faculty whose nature is to acquire information about material, not immaterial things (*S* 1,88,1,2,3).

Question eighty-nine, like question eighty-eight, is devoted to a topic where it is difficult to disentangle philosophical considerations from theological presuppositions. It asks how the soul thinks when it is separated from the body. It was primarily on theological grounds that St Thomas believed in the possibility of an afterlife for the soul after the death of the body. A philosopher who does not share these religious presuppositions will find it unrewarding to follow in detail the account given of the intellectual activity of the disembodied soul. The prior philosophical question is whether there can be any such thing as a disembodied soul, and in particular whether such a notion can be reconciled with the Aristotelian framework within which Aquinas operates. The time has therefore come for us to return to the long-delayed consideration of question seventy-five, where the metaphysical issue is addressed at length, and where Aquinas seeks to establish the coherence of the notion of departed souls as forms denuded of their matter.

11 The nature of the soul

The title of the first article of question seventy-five is surprising: it asks whether the soul is a body. We are so used to the dichotomy of soul and body that the question brings us up short; it seems as strange as to ask whether what is immaterial is material. We may reasonably ask the question whether there is such a thing as a soul – a question to which a materialist would give a negative answer. But surely it would be absurd to give the positive answer, that there are indeed souls, and then go on to add 'but they are just a special kind of body'.

But if we read the article, we see that Aquinas is not working with a concept of 'soul' which has the notion of immateriality built into it. His starting definition is that the soul is 'the first principle of life in living beings'. The soul is whatever makes the difference between animate and inanimate objects. (The Latin word translated 'soul' is *anima*.) It is not something to be taken for granted, but something that needs proof, that this principle of life, this animator, is not a material object.

Life, he says, is manifested chiefly by motion and by consciousness. (This shows that he is thinking here of animal life, though elsewhere he is willing to follow Aristotle in ascribing souls to plants also (S 1,78,1).) Some philosophers have argued that these vital activities demonstrate that the soul must be corporeal; for only a body can cause motion, and only a body can be conscious of bodies, since like is known by like.

Aquinas argues that the opposite is the case: only something which is not a body can be the ultimate principle of motion and consciousness in animals. He concedes that there can be bodily principles of vital activities, that is to say, that the causes of some episodes in the life of an animal may be traced to physical parts of the animal's body. Some vital motions have their origin in the animal's heart, and the form of consciousness which is vision depends on the activity of the animal's eye. But neither the heart nor the eye is a soul. St Thomas is prepared to call each of them a principle of life, but not a root or first principle of life.

The argument that there must be a non-bodily soul is compressed, but it can be expanded thus. If we explain the movement of an animal in terms of the movements of its internal parts, we are explaining the movement of one living body by the movement of another living body. The animal's organs are indeed physical objects; but it is not because they are physical that they cause vital operations, but because they are alive. A dead heart and a dead eye could not perform the functions performed by the living heart and the living eye. Just as we started by asking of the whole animal what made it alive, so we can ask the same question about any organ of the animal which we may find involved in the causation of the animal's behaviour. So for Aquinas, the soul is what answers the question 'What makes it alive?' when asked either of the whole animal or of any of its vital parts.

'The soul', he concludes, 'which is the primary principle of life, is not a body, but an actuality of a body, just as heat, which is the principle of heating, is not a body, but a certain actuality of a body.' The regress of moving parts of the body each in turn moved by other moving parts is brought to an end by the soul which is an unmoved mover (*S* 1,75,1 *ad* 1). The soul is the principle of consciousness not because it actually resembles the material phenomena of which an animal can become aware, but because it has the potentiality to take on an appropriate similarity to them.

Obviously, all this leaves much to be explained. But if we accept Aquinas' argument thus far, we may note immediately that there are three significant limits to what has been established.

First of all, to the extent that the activities of any internal organ of the animal can be explained adequately by the physical properties which it shares with non-living matter, the recursive question 'And what makes this, in its turn, alive?' can no longer be put. Aquinas' argument would collapse if every item in the overt behaviour of an animal could be traced to internal organs which were, in this way, non-vital. Thus Descartes believed that animals were automata whose actions were explained by mechanical causes operating on principles essentially no different from those of clockwork. Descartes's crude mechanicism was soon shown to

be untenable, but none the less, since his time, many biological
processes have been explained in terms of chemical and physical
properties which living tissue shares with non-living matter.
Aquinas' regress argument for the existence of animal souls is
valid only to the extent that there remains a residue of animal
metabolism and behaviour irreducible to the activity of chemical
and physical agents.

Second, even if there are indeed in animals organs whose operation calls for modes of explanation unique to living matter, so
that Aquinas is justified in describing them as 'principles of life', it
is not yet clear that the actuality of life in each organ is one and the
same as the actuality of life in the whole animal. If Aquinas'
argument works at all, it seems to prove not only that a chicken
has a soul, but that a chicken's liver has a soul. So that even if we
accept that animals must have souls, the question remains open
'*How many* souls are there in an animal?' In this case, Aquinas is
well aware that the question remains open, and in the following
question he will devote considerable effort to answering it.

Third, the incorporeality which Aquinas' argument seeks to
establish for the soul is something, so far, far removed from any
kind of spirituality or immortality. The concluding words of the
body of the article, quoted above, compare the non-bodily nature
of the soul to the non-bodily nature of heat. We need not inquire
what particular physical theory of heat Aquinas accepted. In an
obvious sense heat is not a body: the heat of the hot-water bottle
has no size or weight and cannot be carried, dropped, squashed or
punctured as the hot-water bottle can. Similarly, the shape of my
teapot is not a physical object like the teapot; it would not be
included in an inventory of the things in my kitchen. But if it is
only in this sense that a soul is non-bodily, then Aquinas' psychology need not differ from a thoroughgoing materialism; for even
the most hard-bitten materialist may allow into his ontology not
only matter but also the properties of matter.

This third point, too, is something of which Aquinas is well
aware; and indeed in the next article of the question he raises the
issue whether there any souls which – unlike properties of bodies
such as heat – are subsistent entities. In response he argues that
the human soul is not only non-bodily but subsistent, that is has an
independent existence. The argument is difficult to follow, and
before expounding and criticizing it I must set it out in St Thomas'
own words:

> The principle of the operation of the intellect, which we call the human soul, must be said to be an incorporeal and subsistent principle. For it is plain that by his intellect a human being can know the nature of all corporeal things. But to be able to know things, what knows must have nothing of their nature in its own. If it did, what it had in its nature would hinder it from knowing other things, as a sick person's tongue, infected with a bilious and bitter humour, cannot taste anything sweet because everything tastes sour to it. If, then, the intellectual principle had in itself the nature of any corporeal thing, it would not be able to know all corporeal things. But everything that is a body has some determinate nature; and so it is impossible that the intellectual principle should be a body.[1]

Several things are striking about this famous passage. The first is that, in spite of the title of the article, it is not an argument to the effect that the soul is subsistent, but to the effect that it is not a body; but this was already supposed to have been established in the previous article. Second, the principle that like must be known by like, which seemed to be accepted with qualification in the previous article, here seems to be stood on its head: only what is unlike the knower can be known. This principle seems far from self-evident, and in support of it we are offered only the example of taste, explained in accordance with the medieval physiology of the humours.

Without taking issue with that physiology, one might ask what reason there is to think that intellect resembles sense in this respect. And even if we accept the parallel at face value, the argument seems to fail. 'In order to be able to taste all tastes, the tongue must have no taste; *a pari*, in order to understand all corporeal natures, the intellect must have no corporeal nature.' The problem is that the premise is false; the tongue does have a taste – a very pleasant one, as fanciers of ox tongue will agree.

Modern exponents of Aquinas point out that a person who is wearing coloured spectacles is unable to distinguish between the colour of white objects and the colour of objects of the same tint as her spectacles. Aquinas himself, in order to show that the intellect must not only be non-bodily but must also lack a bodily organ, points out that you cannot see the colour of a liquid poured into a coloured glass. But these examples are cases where vision is impeded not by the colour of the seer (a black man can see black surfaces as well as a white man) or by the colour of the organ (blue eyes don't prevent one from seeing the blue lagoon) but by the colour of the medium. And one of the differences between sensation and thought, as Aquinas himself is happy to point out in other places, is that there is not a medium of thought in the same way as there are media of vision or sound.

It is only in the final paragraph of article two that we are offered the argument that the soul must be not only non-bodily, but also subsistent:

> The intellectual principle, therefore, which is called mind or intellect has its own activity in which the body has no share. But nothing can act on its own unless it exists on its own; for only what exists in actuality can act, and the way it acts depends upon the way it exists. Hence we do not say that heat heats, but that the hot body heats. So the human soul, which is called the intellect or mind, is something non-bodily and subsistent.
>
> $(S\ 1,75,2c)^2$

Before evaluating this argument we need to understand its conclusion; we need to know first exactly what is meant by 'subsistent'. The first objection and its answer help a little with this. The objector says that a soul is not a subsistent entity, because it is not a 'this something' – it is not an individual that can be designated. Only the human being, compound of soul and body, is an object of reference of this kind.

In answer, Aquinas distinguishes two ways in which something can fail to be a 'this something'. One way is by being an abstraction, or, as Aquinas says in this context, 'an accident or material form': the shape or size or bark or caninity of a dog is not a 'this something'. The other way is by being a part of something: as a hand or toe is not a 'this something'. In each case, we have an X which is the X *of* something else: the bark of Fido, the toe of St Peter. A soul, he argues, fails to be a 'this something' in the second sense, but it is a 'this something' in the first: it is as concrete an object as a hand or toe. In the second sense, it is true, only the compound of soul and body is a 'this something'.

In the second reply Aquinas relates all this to the definition of 'subsistence', and he introduces at this point a distinction between existence and subsistence. Accidents and material forms, such as heat, neither exist nor subsist of themselves (*per se*). Physical parts like hands and eyes can be said to exist of themselves but do not subsist of themselves. A whole human being is something which both exists and subsists of itself.

In terms of this distinction, is Aquinas saying that the soul subsists of itself, or only that it exists of itself? At the end of the article the reader is left quite unclear. In the *sed contra* a text of Augustine was quoted to support the conclusion that the human mind is a substance, something which subsists. Similarly, the passage from the body of the article quoted above led to the conclusion that the soul was non-bodily and subsistent. Yet in the responses to the objections the soul seems to be placed in the same category as bodily parts such as hands and eyes, which exist of themselves but do not subsist of themselves.

Aquinas' hesitation on this matter comes out particularly clearly in the third objection and its reply. The third objection runs as follows:

> Whatever is subsistent can be described as acting. But the soul cannot be described as acting; because, according to the *De Anima*, to say that the soul senses or thinks is like saying that it weaves or builds. Therefore the soul is not something subsistent.
>
> (*S* 1,75,2 *ad* 3)[3]

The text of the *De Anima* in fact reads as follows: 'To say that the soul gets angry is as if one were to say that the soul weaves or builds a house. Probably it is better not to say that the soul pities or learns or thinks, but that the human being does these things with his soul' (408b13–15). For both Aristotle and Aquinas anger differed from thought in being a phenomenon essentially involving the body, and so the first sentence of the *De Anima* passage might have been taken to be making a restricted point about the relation of the soul to the passions or emotions. But Aquinas' response to the objection is different.

First, he says that Aristotle is here expressing not his own views, but the views of those who believe thought to be a form of motion. It is true that this thesis is the topic of discussion in the relevant part of the *De Anima*, but the words cited come not from the exposition of the opinion to be refuted but from Aristotle's own criticism of that opinion.

Aquinas seems uncomfortable with this answer to the objection, for he quickly moves to give an alternative explanation which depends on the distinction between existence and subsistence, and which concludes with a passage which reads like a paraphrase of the second sentence quoted above from the *De Anima*:

> The operations of parts are attributed to the whole *via* the parts. For we speak of a man seeing with his eye, or feeling with his hand, but not in the same way as a hot body heats with its heat, because strictly speaking the heat in no sense heats. It can be said, therefore, that the soul thinks just as the eye sees, but it is better to say that the human being thinks with his soul.
>
> $(S\ 1,75,2\ ad\ 3)$[4]

From this passage we infer that Aquinas is maintaining that the soul is to be compared with the hand and the eye, and the status being claimed for it is existence and not subsistence.

However, the final sentence, echoing Aristotle, seems to cut the ground from under the argument for independent existence of any kind. For the argument was that the soul must have an existence because it has an independent operation, namely thinking. But it now appears that to say 'the soul thinks' is an insufficiently rigorous mode of expression. What really thinks is the human being, not the soul. So even if we grant that thought involves no bodily organ,[5] the only entity whose independent existence can be inferred is the human being, the thinker. The comparison between the soul and the hand leads to the same conclusion. A hand can be an object of reference, and not all statements about hands are statements about the whole person whose hands they are; but hands do not have separate existences and cannot continue to exist, as hands, once the whole body has died.

But is it really appropriate to compare a soul with a hand or an eye, rather than with the heat of a hot body? Some idioms seem to support the contrast Aquinas wishes to make. We do say that we see with our eyes and feel with our hands, but if my body heat melts the ice-cream as I carry it home in my hands, we do not say 'I melted the ice-cream with my heat'. But the contrast of idiom seems to be based on the contrast between the voluntariness of looking and feeling, and the non-voluntariness of giving off heat. It does not seem to have anything to do with the fact that heat is, as Aquinas puts it, 'a material form'.

We may indeed wonder what right Aquinas has to use such an expression. Given that matter and form are standardly introduced as a contrasting pair, is not 'material form' something of an oxymoron like 'triangular quadrilateral'? The paradoxical nature of the expression alerts us to the fact that in these crucial texts which analyse the nature of the soul there are two different contrasts in play: one between the concrete and the abstract, and the other between the physical and the non-physical. Words such as 'material' or 'bodily' may be used in different contexts to mark either of these contrasts.

The first two articles of question seventy-five in a manner cancel each other out. The first argues to the conclusion that the soul is incorporeal in the sense that it is abstract and not concrete: it is not a body but an actuality of a body. The second argues to the conclusion that the soul is incorporeal in the sense that it is a non-physical part of a human being: it is an agent with no bodily organ. But an agent cannot be an abstraction, and what is abstract cannot be a part of what is concrete.

The hand and the eye are parts of the human body, and what is part of a body is itself bodily. If a human being is a human body, then he cannot have a part which is non-bodily; if he has a soul, it is not as part of himself. Elsewhere, as we shall see, this is the position which Aquinas takes.[6] In question seventy-five he speaks as if a human being is not a human body, but a composite of two parts, one corporeal, and the other incorporeal. No doubt the notions of 'whole' and 'part' are flexible enough to cover non-bodily entities as well as bodies, and perhaps even to straddle the difference between the two: we may after all speak without absurdity of a constitution as having written and unwritten parts. The difficulty is not in the notion of an entity with physical and non-physical parts, but in the notion of an entity with concrete and abstract parts.

We shall return to this difficulty in the next chapter, when we consider Aquinas' exposition of his theory that the human soul is the form of the human body. For the present, let us follow Aquinas in his exposition of the two-part theory of the human being, in the fourth article of the question which asks whether a human being is to be identified with his soul. The text in the *sed contra* quotes Augustine as supporting the view that a human being is neither the soul alone, nor the body alone, but body and soul together.

It is, according to Aquinas, a Platonic view that the real human being is the soul (the 'inward man' in St Paul's phrase) which makes use of the body as an instrument. But it might be thought that it followed also from Aquinas' own line of argument that a soul was a human being. A soul is a subsistent entity, he has argued, a substance. It is also human, and it is also individual. But what is an individual human substance if it is not a human being (*S* 1,75,4,2)? To this he can answer, consistenly with article two, that the same argument would prove that a hand or a foot was a human being: it is an individual, substantial entity which is human. But neither hand nor foot nor soul is a complete human being: and that is what is at issue in this article (*S* 1,75,4 *ad* 2).

In the body of the article, Aquinas has two different targets. The first is the Platonist who thinks that a full human life is possible without a body, and that all human activities have the soul alone as their agent. Against this view, Aquinas insists that a human being is not just a thinker, but a perceiver: sense-perception, though not peculiar to human beings, is a human activity no less than intellectual thought. Plato before Aquinas, and Descartes after Aquinas, thought that sense-experience was possible in the absence of a body; but Aquinas is firmly and rightly convinced that this view is erroneous. 'Since, then, sense-experience is an activity of a human being, even though not restricted to humans, it is clear that a human being is not a soul alone but is a compound of soul and body.'[7]

Aquinas' other target is a more subtle opinion. According to this second view, being human is the same thing as having a soul; but any actual human being is not just a soul, but also has a body, even though having a body is not part of what it is to be a human being. No proponent of this opinion is mentioned, but it is generally taken that Aquinas has Avicenna in view.

> Some have said that only form belongs to the concept of a species, while matter is a part of the individual and not of the species. But this cannot be true. For what belongs to the nature of a species is what is included in its definition. In physical things the definition includes not the form alone, but matter as well as form, so that matter is part of the species in physical things; not some designated piece of matter, which is the principle of individuation, but matter in general. It is part of the concept of *this* man that he should have *this* soul and *this* flesh and *these* bones; it is part of the concept of man that he should have a soul and flesh and bones.

> (*S* 1,75,4c)[8]

Once again we have a disconcerting disdain for distinctions between abstract and concrete. In accordance with Aquinas' general
theory of individuation, Socrates is the individual he is because he
is a particular concrete chunk of matter. The same goes for any
other human being: he will be one or other concrete chunk of
matter. Averroes will not, so far, disagree. But Aquinas wants to
go further: being material is actually part of what it is to be a
human being. But the contrast between a chunk of matter and the
property of being material – a contrast between something concrete and something abstract – is misleadingly understated as a
contrast between designated matter and matter in general. Being
material or corporeal is, in fact, like any other property, a form.

What Aquinas is really arguing against Averroes is that the
property of being material, the form of corporeality, is something
included in humanity, not something separate from it and inessential to it. This is ground which will be extensively revisited in
question seventy-six. We may surely agree with Aquinas against
Averroes that human beings are, by definition, bodily beings.

This does, of course, raise difficulties for Aquinas' belief in an
afterlife. Aquinas undoubtedly believed that each human being
had an immortal soul, which could survive the death of the body
and continue to think and will in the period before the eventual
resurrection of the body to which he looked forward. None the
less, Aquinas did not believe in a self which was distinct from the
body, nor did he think that disembodied souls were persons.

This is made clear in a striking passage in his commentary on the
First Epistle to the Corinthians. Commenting on the passage 'If in
this life only we have hope in Christ we are of all men most
miserable', St Thomas wrote:

> A human being naturally desires his own salvation; but the soul,
> since it is part of the body of a human being, is not a whole
> human being, and my soul is not I; so even if a soul gains
> salvation in another life, that is not I or any human being.[9]

It is remarkable that St Thomas says not just that the soul is only a
part of a human being, but that it is only part of *the body* of a
human being. Commonly he uses 'soul' and 'body' as correlatives,
and often he writes as if soul and body are related to each other as
the form and the matter of the Aristotelian hylomorphism. But the
formulation which he uses in this passage is in fact the more

correct one from the hylomorphic standpoint: the human being is a body which like other mutable bodies is composed of matter and form; the soul, which is the form of the living body, is one part of the body, and the matter is another part of it, with 'part' used in the very special sense which is appropriate in this context.

What is most clear from the passage is that St Thomas refuses to identify the disembodied soul, even a beatified disembodied soul, with any self or ego. According to St Thomas what I am, what you are, what everyone else is is nothing less than a human being. He refuses to identify the individual with the individual's soul, as Descartes was to do.

Some of Aquinas' predecessors and contemporaries, such as the Muslim Ibn Gebirol, and the Franciscan St Bonaventure, took the idea of the soul as a concrete object so seriously that they maintained that it was itself composed of form and matter in the way in which, according to hylomorphic theory, bodies are. Souls were not, however, made out of the same matter as bodies – otherwise they would *be* bodies – but were made out of a special, spiritual, matter.

Is the notion of spiritual matter absurd, involving a contradiction in terms, like the notion of a square circle? No doubt it is, if one thinks of extension and tangibility as the essential elements of matter. But those who believed in spiritual matter insisted that matter is essentially potentiality: matter is the ability to have properties and to undergo change. The soul can have properties, such as knowledge and virtue, and it can undergo change, passing, for example, from ignorance to knowledge and from vice to virtue. Therefore it must contain matter, the potentiality for change (*S* 1,75,5,2).

Aquinas rejected the theory that the soul was made of spiritual matter, but he did not treat the notion as a plain absurdity. He felt obliged to develop arguments against it, and he went to some lengths to spell out the truths which the theory was a misguided attempt to express.

First, he points out that the theory is incompatible with his own view that the soul is pure form – a view which he will spell out more fully in the succeeding question, seventy-six. He does not, however, go on consistently with this Aristotelian theory to reject his opponents' argument by saying that strictly speaking it is not the soul, but the human being, which passes from ignorance to knowledge. Instead, he accepts that the soul does so, but seeks to show that it does so in a way which is incompatible with the containment of matter.

> Each thing is known in so far as its form is in the knower. The intellectual soul's knowledge is pure knowledge of a thing's nature; knowledge, for instance, of stone simply *qua* stone. Thus the pure form of stone is in the intellectual soul in accordance with its own formal concept. The intellectual soul, therefore, is pure form, not something composed of matter and form. For if the intellectual soul were composed of matter and form, the forms of things would be received in it as individual. In that case it would not have knowledge of anything except singulars, as is the case with the sensory powers, which receive the forms of things in a bodily organ. For matter is the principle of individuation of forms.
>
> (*S* 1,75,5c)[10]

The way in which the intellect passes from ignorance to knowledge is by acquiring ideas (*species intelligibiles*). But the ideas that get lodged in the mind are universal; whereas if there were matter in the mind, they would become individuated. Hence the way in which a form is present in the mind is different from the way in which forms are received in matter (*S* 1,75,5 *ad* 1 and *ad* 2).

What are we to think of this argument? 'Prime matter receives individual forms, the intellect receives pure forms', says Aquinas. That is to say, the shape of the Great Pyramid is *its* shape, and not the shape of any other pyramidal object; but my intellectual idea of a pyramid is the idea purely of pyramid and not the idea of any particular pyramid. So far, so good: but might not the defender of spiritual matter say that Aquinas is looking in the wrong place for the individuality of an idea? Sure, my idea is not the idea of an individual object; but it *is* an idea belonging to an individual subject: it is *my* idea and not your idea or Cleopatra's idea. It is individuated by its presence in my mind rather than another mind; and is this not parallel to the individuation of a shape by its inhering in one parcel of matter rather than another?

It seems, in fact, that if one is prepared to regard the soul as being in any way a concrete entity, and if one defines materiality not as extension or tangibility but simply as potentiality, there is no good reason to deny that the soul is composed of matter and form. The real weakness which Aquinas sees in the position of his opponents is that they are unwilling to make the necessary distinctions between different kinds of potentiality. In the answers to the objections in question seventy-five he goes some way to remedy this.

In the Aristotelian system there were three different instances of the contrast potentiality vs actuality: substance vs accident, matter vs form and essence vs existence. Substance is what has the potentiality for taking on various accidental forms; matter is what has the potentiality for taking on various substantial forms. The forms which the soul takes on when it changes are accidental forms, such as knowledge and virtue; they are not substantial forms, because the soul cannot turn into something else, as an animal body does when it dies and decays. So the soul cannot be said to be matter; but it can be said to be a substance, as Aquinas agrees.

What of the contrast 'essence/existence'? To the claim that if the soul were a form without matter it would be pure and infinite actuality, Aquinas replies as follows:

> God alone, who is his own being, is pure and infinite actuality. In intellectual substances there is a compounding of actuality and potentiality, but not of matter and form, but of form and the being in which it shares. Accordingly some say that there is a compound consisting of that which has being and the being which it has.
>
> $$(S \ 1,75,5 \ ad \ 4)^{11}$$

Fortunately we do not at this point have to investigate the tangled topic of Being in order to settle whether the account here adumbrated by Aquinas can be stated in a fully coherent and intelligible form. All that is necessary to note here is that, in Aquinas' view, the contrast between matter and form is not the appropriate one to use in trying to differentiate between the metaphysical status of a creature which owes its existence to a creator, and a God whose existence has no external cause.

In the sixth article Aquinas addresses the question whether the soul is immortal, though he does not use the word 'immortal' but asks instead whether the soul is corruptible, that is to say, whether it can decompose or pass away. Two pages seem little enough to devote to an issue of such moment: but in the preceding articles the ground has been well prepared for the position he takes up.

The main arguments he presents against immortality, surprisingly, are texts from Scripture. Such texts more commonly appear in the *sed contra*, setting the tone for Aquinas' own thesis. But in this case there are two important texts from the Old Testament which need to be taken into account by any defender of the immortality of the soul. 'That which befalleth the sons of men befalleth beasts', said the Preacher. 'Even one thing befalleth them: as the one dieth, so dieth the other; yea, they have all one breath; so that a man hath no preeminence above a beast: for all is vanity. All go unto one place; all are of the dust, and all turn to dust again' (Ecclesiastes 3,19–20). And in the deutero-canonical book of Wisdom Aquinas read 'We were born out of nothing, and after this we shall be as though we had never been' (Wisdom 2,2).

Despite these texts, Aquinas argues that there is no way in which the soul can decompose or pass away. Some things cease to exist when other things decompose: this is the case with accidental forms. Thus, a candle's colour or shape no longer exist once the candle itself has been consumed. It is the same with substantial forms where these are not self-subsistent: thus an animal's soul passes away when the animal itself decomposes. But a human soul, it has been argued, is self-subsistent; and this means that it can pass away only by decomposing itself. But, as has been argued, it has no parts to decompose into.

Decomposition occurs when a piece of matter loses a form which it previously had. But it has just been argued that the soul contains no matter: being itself a form, it cannot lose form. A subsistent form cannot cease to be.

Even if the argument of the previous article were mistaken, and the soul were a compound of matter and form, it would still – Aquinas argues – be incapable of decay or decomposition. For decomposition is transition from one state of matter to a contrary state which is incompatible with it. There is more than one way in which a material entity may be incapable of decomposing in this manner.

The heavenly bodies, Aquinas believed – the sun and moon and stars – were indeed material; but none the less they were incapable of decay, because of the particular kind of matter they were made of – a unique and sublime matter which had no capacity to take on any different, incompatible, substantial form. The intellect, on the other hand, whether or not we think of it as material, is incapable of decay for the opposite reason. It is not that it is incapable of taking on a contrary form and thus passing out of existence: it can take on contrary forms simultaneously, while continuing to exist unchanged in its own nature. Health may be incompatible with sickness, but knowledge of health is compatible with knowledge of sickness, and indeed according to a familiar Aristotelian slogan, it is the very same thing. *Eadem est scientia oppositorum*: to know what it is to be F is *eo ipso* to know what it is not to be F.

In response to the Scripture texts, Aquinas insists that there is all the difference in the world between animals and humans, because the latter can think intellectual thoughts and the former cannot. The quotations must be taken not as the expression of the sacred authors' own opinions, but as opinions of the fools they were attacking. This is indeed clear in Wisdom, where the words are expressly attributed to the godless; and the quotation from Ecclesiastes can be capped with one in the opposite sense from the same text: 'Then shall the dust return to the earth as it was: and the spirit shall return unto God who gave it' (Ecclesiastes 12,7).

Aquinas' argument is not meant to show that the soul will survive for ever. He believed that it was, and always would be, within God's power to annihilate a soul, to return it, as it were, to the nothingness from which it had been created. But a cessation of existence of this kind, though logically possible, would not be a death. Hence the soul was incapable of death, and in that sense immortal, despite God's omnipotent power to destroy it (*S* 1,75,6 c and *ad* 2).

The argument for immortality stands or falls with the argument for self-subsistence.[12] I have argued that that argument involves a confusion between abstract and concrete, and the same confusion, I believe, vitiates the argument for immortality. But the exact nature of the confusion will only become clear after we have examined, in the next chapter, Aquinas' full-scale treatment, in question seventy-six, of the relationship between the soul and the body.[13]

12 Mind and body

The long first article of question seventy-six aims to work out in fuller detail the relationship between Aquinas' teaching on the soul, as set out in question seventy-five, and the Aristotelian theory of matter and form. The positive discussion of this issue takes its start from the traditional definition of a human being, 'man is a rational animal'. In the scholastic jargon, animal is the genus, man is the species, and 'rational' indicates the specific difference which marks out the species within the genus. But a specific difference is, according to Aristotelian theory, a form. Therefore, the intellectual principle which is denoted by the word 'rational' must be the human being's form.

That is the brief, programmatic argument in the *sed contra*. Aquinas' substantial argument for the identification of soul and form, in the body of the article, runs as follows:

> We must say that the intellect, which is the principle of intellectual activity, is the form of the human body. For that with which first something acts is a form of that to which the action is attributed, such as that with which first a body is made healthy is health, and that with which first a soul knows is knowledge, so that health is a form of the body and knowledge is a form of the soul. The reason for this is that nothing acts unless it is in actuality, and that by which something is actual is that with which it acts.
>
> $(S\ 1,76,1)^1$

I have translated with barbaric literalism, because it is difficult to give a flowing translation that is not tendentious. The crucial expression is 'that with which first something acts' (*id quo primo aliquid operatur*). The Latin ablative case (and the Greek dative case, in the Aristotelian text which underlies this passage of Aquinas) is the case used for a tool or instrument or organ by means of which an agent does something. It commonly corresponds to the English word 'with'. I cut the bread *with* a knife, push a boat off *with* a paddle; Nelson could see *with* his good eye; it is wise to feel the heat of the bathwater *with* one's toe.

Clearly, many of the things which we do are done by means of instruments or organs in this way. But it seems an unnecessary generalization to say that whatever is done is done *with* something. Some actions, it seems natural to think, are done *with* things; others are just done. Hot bodies heat other bodies, and they heat things because they are hot; but it seems odd to say that they heat *with* their heat. Again, there are many things which I know, but I don't know them *with* anything. But Aquinas here seems to be assuming that wherever an agent does something by virtue of possessing a certain property, then it acts *with* that property. It appears that on the view presented here, the things which we would normally say we do things with – knives and paddles – are only that with which secondly we do things. The items with which first we do things are all items related to the actions in the internal manner in which health is related to being healthy and knowledge is related to knowing.

Aquinas says that 'nothing acts unless it is in actuality, and that by which something is actual is that with which it acts'. If we understand this as meaning that nothing makes something else F unless it is itself F, and the F-ness by which it is itself F is the F-ness by which it acts, then it is not too difficult to apply the theorem to the actions of heating, cooling, wetting and drying which were the paradigms of activity in Aristotelian physics. Nothing heats unless it is hot, and the heat which makes it hot is the heat with which it heats other things; nothing wets unless it is wet, and the wetness which makes it wet is the wetness with which it wets other things. These remarks seem to be broadly true, even if not particularly informative.

There is a problem, however, in speaking of an agent's acting with, or by virtue of, its form. The problem is not simply one of idiom, Greek, Latin or English. What is questionable is that the language makes a misleading assimilation between the relationship of an agent to an external instrument, such as a spade, and the relationship of an agent to a form, such as knowledge. The one relation is a contingent one, an empirical matter: digging is possible, even if difficult, if one hasn't a spade. But it is a matter of tautology that one cannot know without having knowledge. There is danger of a confusion here, a confusion of which, as we shall see, it is difficult wholly to acquit Aquinas.

If we know with our knowledge, then *a pari* do we not live with our life? What Aquinas actually says is that we live with our soul:

> It is clear that the first thing with which a body lives is the soul. Life is manifested in different activities at different levels of life, but the soul is that with which first we perform each one of the activities of life. The soul is the first thing with which we nourish ourselves and exercise our senses and move from place to place, and likewise the first thing with which we think. So this principle with which first we think, whether it is called the intellect or the intellectual soul, is the form of the body.
>
> $(S\ 1,76,1)^2$

There seems to be a difficulty in reconciling the statement here that the soul is the principle with which first we think, and the statement quoted above that knowledge is that with which first the soul knows. The reconciliation seems to be that the human being acts by means of its soul, and the soul acts by means of its knowledge.

Aquinas now turns to a different approach to establishing the thesis that the intellect is the form of the body, taking as his premise the proposition that each of us is conscious that he himself both senses and thinks. In human beings sensation and thought are certainly self-conscious activities: but it is not clear what exactly, in the absence of very special circumstances, is the content of the judgement 'It is I, and not someone else, who is doing this sensing and thinking.' (What would it be like for this judgement to be mistaken?) Now if Socrates knows that he is thinking, is it all of him or a part of him that is doing the thinking? It cannot be all of him that is doing the thinking, for since thinking is a non-bodily activity, that would mean that he had no body. But since he knows that he is also sensing, he must have a body, since sensation is impossible without a body. His body is a part of him, and so his intellect cannot be the whole of him. Therefore, it must be a part of him that is doing the thinking, a part which is linked to his body.

How is it linked to his body? Aquinas considers three possibilities: as knower to object, as cause to effect, and as form to substance. All of these possibilities had been canvassed by Aristotelian predecessors or contemporaries of his.

Suppose we say, first, that Socrates' intellect is linked to Socrates' body because that body provides the immediate objects of its awareness, for example, images or patterns in the brain. But it cannot be that which makes the intellect in question be the intellect of Socrates. In such a case Socrates would be what was being thought about, but would not be what was doing the thinking. If a fresco provides the object of my vision, that does not mean that the fresco is doing any seeing; equally, providing an object for thought does not suffice for being a thinker.

Suppose we say instead, then, that Socrates' intellect causes the behaviour of his body, and that is what makes it possible to attribute the activity of the intellect to Socrates himself. Aquinas gives several arguments against this view, including the following. Let us turn from the thinker Socrates to the carpenter Joseph: if Joseph saws a piece of wood, he causes the motion of the saw. But we cannot attribute this activity of Joseph to the saw; or if we do, we simply mean that the saw was an instrument of Joseph. So if we were, in a parallel fashion, to attribute thinking to the body of Socrates, it would be as an instrument of the intellect. But it is common ground among Aristotelians that the intellect has no bodily organ.

Suppose that Socrates and some intellect together made up some compound, then Socrates could not be said to think; for though the action of a part can be ascribed to a whole, the action of a part cannot be ascribed to another part: when my eye sees something, I see it, but my hand doesn't. If, on the other hand, Socrates were himself a compound of an intellect plus bodily elements which were related to it only by the relation of cause to effect, then Socrates would not really be a unity. Two effects which share a relation to a cause are not thereby parts of a single entity, any more than Joseph's saw and Joseph's hammer are part of a composite whole in virtue of both being acted on by Joseph.

Note that Aquinas does not deny, indeed he affirms, that the soul does move the body. What he denies is that this relationship between soul and body is sufficient to explain their unity. The motion of the body by the soul is the consequence, and not the foundation, of the unity of the whole human being of which body and soul are both parts.

We are left, Aquinas says, with the conclusion that what makes a man's thought *his* thought is that the source or principle of the thought is his form, the form of his body. And it is the capacity to think that makes a human being human, for that is the activity which distinguishes men from animals. But what makes an F an F is its form; so the intellectual soul, the principle of thinking, is the human form.

In this article, as in many others, there seems to be a tension between two different ways of understanding the notion of form. First, there is what we may call the abstract notion of form. Whenever there is a true sentence on the pattern 'A is F', we can speak of the form of F-ness; an accidental form or a substantial form as the case may be. If A is hot, there is such a thing as the hotness of A; if A is an animal, there is such a thing as the animality of A. Thus, the hotness, or heat, of a hot body is what makes it hot, and that is an example of an accidental form. The substantial form in a human being may likewise be introduced as being, truistically, that by which a man is a man, or that which makes a man a man. In each of these cases the 'makes' is the 'makes' of formal causality, as when we say that it is a certain shape which makes a piece of metal a key, or a certain structure which makes a molecule a DNA molecule. If the soul is a form in this sense, then it is no more a concrete object than a shape or a structure is.

But besides the abstract notion of form, there is a notion of form as an agent. In these passages it is clear that Aquinas thinks of the human soul as being causally responsible for the various activities which make up a human life. And here the causality is efficient causality, the sort of causality for which nowadays the word 'cause' is commonly reserved, as when we are told that it is the yeast that causes the bread to rise or that DNA molecules cause the synthesis of proteins. It is this kind of relationship that is suggested when we are told that the soul is the principle of life. Aquinas speaks of the soul as 'moving' the body, and 'move' is the word which is used to signify efficient causality as opposed to formal causality.

The two notions of form seem to be different from each other and impossible to combine, without confusion, into a single notion. However, in the present article Aquinas goes as far as he is ever able to do to present the notion of the soul as form in a coherent and unconfused manner. Thus he presents, and attempts to answer, two objections which seek to press precisely the issues which cause the intellectual discomfort just described.

Thus the fourth objection runs:

> What has being of itself is not united to a body as form, because
> a form is that by which something is, and thus the very being of
> a form does not belong to the form in itself. But the intellectual
> principle has being in itself, and is self-subsistent, as said above.
> Therefore it is not united to the body as its form.
>
> (S 1,76,1,5)[3]

What is here said of form is sound Aristotelian doctrine: the
existence of a form is simply its inherence in its subject; for A's
F-ness to exist is simply for A to be F. This is in full accord with the
abstract notion of form, and the objection spells out the difficulty
of reconciling this with the concrete notion of the soul as a self-
subsistent entity.

Aquinas' answer runs:

> The soul communicates to bodily matter the being in which it
> itself subsists; from this matter and the intellectual soul there
> comes into existence a unity such that the being of the com-
> pound whole is the being also of the soul. This does not happen
> in other forms which are not subsistent.
>
> (S 1,76,1 *ad* 5)[4]

This answer quite fails to meet the objection. Perhaps it can be
rephrased so as to eliminate the suggestion of the pre-existence of
the soul, which fits Platonism better than Thomism. But it presupposes the very possibility which the objector denied, namely the
possibility of subsistent forms.

The sixth objection is based on the principle that being united to
matter is something essential to a form. That is what form is, the
actuality of matter; and if it were not that, then the union of form
and matter would be something accidental rather than essential.
Hence, a form cannot be without its own matter; but the soul,
according to Aquinas, cannot pass away, and therefore survives
the death of the body. Hence the soul cannot be a form.

Aquinas' answer appeals to medieval physics. Varying his
example slightly, we can report him as arguing that a tendency to
fall is no less essential to a heavy body than union with a body is to
the soul. Heavy bodies may be held up, but they retain a tendency
to fall. Similarly, he says, a soul can continue to exist after
separation from the body, but retains a tendency to embodiment.

Again, the answer misses the force of the objection. The impossibility of a form without matter is a logical impossibility, not a matter of physics. Aquinas' answer is no more credible than that of someone who defended the possibility of square circles on the ground that even if a circle became a square, it would retain a tendency to circularity.

Aquinas' last word, in the body of the article, on the relation between form and matter is this:

> The nobler a form is the more it dominates bodily matter, the less it is immersed in it, and the more it surpasses it in activity and capacity. Thus, we see that the form of a compound has activities which are not caused by the properties of the elements which make it up. The higher up we go in the scale of forms, the more we find the power of a form to surpass the elemental matter, the plant forms more than the forms of metals, and the animal soul more than the plant soul. But the human soul is the highest in the scale of nobility of forms. Hence by its power it so surpasses bodily matter that it has an activity and capacity in which bodily matter has no share; and this power is called the intellect.
>
> (*S* 1,76,1)[5]

As so often in Aquinas, we find here a mixture of elements, some of which seem astonishingly contemporary, while others seem irremediably archaic. The claim that chemical properties are not reducible to physical ones, and that biological activities are not explicable in chemical terms, is one which has often been repeated by philosophers well acquainted with the progress of science since the thirteenth century. But the appeal to a hierarchy of nobility among forms is difficult to restate in a way which will strike a chord among twentieth-century philosophers of any school. The problem with forms free of matter is not a question of value, but a question of logic.

Aquinas regarded the souls of human beings, and indeed of all living things, as particular instances of substantial forms. As an Aristotelian he considered that animals and vegetables had souls no less than human beings: a soul was simply the principle of life in organic living beings, and there are many non-human organisms. The special privilege of human beings was not their possession of a soul, but their possession of a rational or intellectual soul. Now human beings grow and take nourishment, just as vegetables do; they see and taste and run and sleep just as animals do. Does this mean that they have a vegetable and animal soul as well as a human soul?

Many of Aquinas' contemporaries answered this question in the affirmative. They held that in the human being there was not just a single form, the intellectual soul, but also animal and vegetable souls; and for good measure some of them added a further form, a form which made a human being a bodily being. This was a 'form of corporeality' which human beings had in common with stocks and stones just as they had a sensitive soul in common with animals and a vegetative soul in common with plants.

Aquinas rejected this proliferation of substantial forms. He maintained that in a human being there was only a single substantial form: the rational soul. It was that soul which controlled the animal and vegetable functions of human beings, and it was that soul which made a human body the kind of body it was: there was no substantial form of corporeality making a human body bodily. If there had been a plurality of forms, he argued, one could not say that it was one and the same human being who thought, loved, felt, heard, ate, drank, slept and had a certain weight and size. When a human being died, there was a substantial change; and, as in any substantial change, there was nothing in common to the two terms of the change other than prime matter.

The second and third articles of question seventy-six seek to establish that there is a one–one correspondence between human bodies and human souls. The second article rejects the suggestion that there might be a single soul for many bodies; and the third article rejects the suggestion that there might be many souls in a single body. It might be thought that the one–one correspondence had already been established in the previous discussion.

This is not entirely true, however. The first article, one might say, established that a human being is a marriage of body and soul. But marriage can be polygamous or polyandrous. A familiar iconographical tradition represents souls as being female (*anima*, after all, is feminine in Latin). If we follow this tradition, and think corresondingly of the body as being male, then we can say that the second article is directed against the polyandrous view of the body–soul relationship, and the third article is directed against the polygamous view. The issue has been settled in the first article only to the extent that the underlying model of body–soul union has been a monogamous one.

The discussion of the polyandrous view (the view of the

Averroists) contains much ingenious argument on either side. The large number of objections and replies show that the issue was a matter of lively debate in Aquinas' time. To refute the polyandrous view, Aquinas seeks to show that however the mind–body relationship is conceived, it will have unacceptable consequences if we suppose a single intellect to be united to many bodies. In every case, he argues, if you and I share the same soul we will turn out to be the same person.

We can illustrate his line of argument in the case of the theory which he regards as the least implausible of the opposing views:

> My thinking might differ from your thinking because of the difference between our phantasms: I have one image of stone and you have another. But this could only be so if the phantasm, in its distinct individuality, was the form of the receptive intellect. The same agent does indeed perform different actions when differently informed: for instance, when two different forms inform one and the same eye there are two distinct acts of seeing. But the phantasm is not the form of the receptive intellect, but the intelligible idea which is abstracted from the phantasms. And from however many phantasms of the same kind only one intelligible idea is abstracted by a single intellect. . . . If therefore there was only a single intellect for all men, the variety of phantasms in different men could not make any difference between the thinking of one man and the thinking of another.
>
> (*S* 1,76,2)[6]

The most telling of the arguments put forward on the other side is as follows. If what individuates souls is their one–one correspondence with different bodies, then when the bodies die there would only be a single soul, since what made the difference between souls has now disappeared. To this Aquinas replied simply that if you can accept the continued existence of the disembodied soul, you should be able also to accept the continued individuation of the disembodied soul (*S* 1,76,2 and *ad* 2). Perhaps this is correct. But the conclusion to draw might be that one should rethink one's acceptance of disembodied existence; for the consideration of disembodied individuation brings out in a particularly vivid way the difficulties inherent in the original notion. No doubt, in terms of our matrimonial analogy, Aquinas could point out that Tom's widow and Dick's widow and Harry's widow are three different widows, in spite of Tom, Dick and Harry all being in their graves. But to this the reply must be that women are individuated by their husbands *as wives*, not as human beings.

Article three moves on from polyandry to polygamy: can a single human being have more than one soul? The supporters of the polygamous view are not Muslim thinkers, but Christian ones; and indeed the theory was officially promulgated by successive Archbishops of Canterbury, after Aquinas' death. Aquinas' argument for the single soul view is simple: it is that if a human being had three different souls, he would be three different animals. His consistent principle is: one substance, one substantial form. On the basis of this Aquinas goes on to argue, in article four, that not only can a human being not have more than one soul, but it is also impossible to have any extra substantial forms (for example, the forms of the chemical substances in the body) in addition to the soul.

If there were some other substantial form pre-existing in matter when the intellectual soul was joined to the body, then the soul would merely be introducing an accidental change into the body, and not giving it existence as the kind of thing it is. Likewise, the departure of the soul would not be the cessation of the life of the human being, but merely an insubstantial change.

> So we must say that there is no substantial form in a human being other than the intellectual soul, and that just as that soul has the power to do all that the sensory and the nutritive soul can do, so too it has the powers to effect whatever in other beings is done by the more elementary forms.
>
> $(S\ 1,76,4)^7$

A point which is closely connected to this one is the thesis that the whole soul is in every part of the human body. Descartes believed that the soul was united to the body at a very particular point: the pineal gland. Many modern thinkers, if they are willing to talk of the soul at all, conceive it as having its seat in the brain, or in the central nervous system. For Aquinas the soul is no more in the brain than it is in the big toe.

> A substantial form is the form not just of the whole, but of every one of its parts. Since a whole is made up of parts, if the form of the whole were not what kept in existence the particular parts, it would merely be a pattern or structure, like the design

of a house; and such a form is an accidental rather than a substantial form. But the soul is a substantial form, and hence it must be the form and actuality not only of the whole but of every part. That is why when the soul departs, what is left is not a human or an animal any more, except by a figure of speech, in the same way as a picture or a sculpture may be; and the same holds, as Aristotle says, for hand and eye and for flesh and bone. This is exhibited in the fact that no part of the body continues to function after the soul has departed.

$$(S\ 1,76,8)[8]$$

Though the whole soul is in every part of the body, not all of the powers of the soul can be exercised in any given part of the body; in respect of its power of sight, Aquinas says, it is in the eye, in respect of its power of hearing it is in the ear and so on. The soul, being immaterial, cannot be divided into parts, as a body can; but it can be looked on as a whole consisting of parts, in the sense that it has many different powers, and these powers can be regarded as its parts.

Question seventy-seven, which is the last we shall consider, discusses the relationship between the soul and its powers, asking how many powers there are in the soul, how powers are individuated one from another, and what relationships they have to each other.

The notion of power, or ability, is one of great importance in many areas of philosophy, and in a study of Aquinas' metaphysics would deserve a much longer treatment than we have room for here. Rather than follow the detailed course of the argument of question seventy-seven, I will restrict myself to making a few general points.

Powers are specified by their exercises (*S* 1,77,3). That is to say, you can only understand what the power to ø is if you know what øing is. One power differs from another if its exercises and its objects differ: for instance, the ability to swim is different from the ability to fly, because swimming is different from flying; and the ability to bake bread is different from the ability to bake biscuits, because bread is different from biscuits.

This gives us one basis for the individuation of powers, for counting how many powers there are. Your ability to speak French is a different ability from your ability to speak German, because the exercises of the two abilities are different. But there is another way in which we might count powers. Your ability to swim is distinct from my ability to swim – not because (as may well be the case) you swim better than I do, but because one ability is your ability and the other ability is my ability, and you and I are two different people. So we have to consider, if we want to count powers, not just the exercises of the powers, but the possessors of the powers.

But though abilities are individuated by their exercises and their possessors, they have to be distinguished from each. The exercise of an ability will be a datable and clockable event: you spoke French for ten minutes last Tuesday. Your ability to speak French is not similarly datable and clockable, but is a more or less enduring state. The possessor of an ability is what *has* the ability: I, for instance, possess the ability to speak English and to ride a bicycle. The possessor of an ability must be distinguished not only from the ability itself, but also from other powers or abilities which may be hierarchically related to the ability in question. It is I, and not my locomotive power, who have the ability to swim.

Thus far, I believe, Aquinas would agree with everything I have said about abilities, and at a number of places in the course of question seventy-seven he makes similar points about the exercise and objects of abilities (*actus et obiecta*) and about the possessors (*subiecta*) of abilities (for example, *S* 1,77,2 and *ad* 2; *S* 1,77,3c; *S* 1,77,5c).

In addition to an ability and its exercise and its possessor we may introduce the notion of the *vehicle* of an ability. The vehicle of an ability is the physical ingredient or structure in virtue of which the possessor of an ability possesses the ability and is able to exercise it. Thus, the vehicle of whisky's power to inebriate is the alcohol it contains, and the vehicle of my key's ability to open the garage door is the shape of its bit. This is a distinction which Aquinas does not make; though he frequently distinguishes between an ability and its organ, which is a particular kind of vehicle: roughly speaking, a part of a vehicle subject to voluntary control.

There are two temptations which beset philosophers when they are considering powers or abilities. On the one hand, there is the temptation to deny the reality of powers by attempting to reduce them to something else, whether to their exercises (as Hume tried to do) or to their vehicles (as Descartes tried to do). On the other hand, there is the temptation to give excessive substantiality to powers and treat them as substances or parts or ingredients of substances. This second error of the hypostatization of abilities is illustrated by the Andersen fairy-tale in which the goblin takes the housewife's gift of the gab and gives it to the water-butt.

These errors are manifested vividly in philosophical accounts of the intellectual powers of human beings. Behaviourists, when they reduce the mind to its exhibition in behaviour, are reductionists of the first kind, who attempt to reduce powers to their exercises. Materialists, when they identify the mind with the brain, are reductionists of the second kind, who confuse powers with their vehicles.

Aquinas' account of mind clearly avoids either of these pitfalls on the reductionist side. But does he avoid the trap on the opposite side? Is not, in fact, his belief that it was possible for the soul to survive the body a particularly glaring example of the hypostatization of powers?

There are various ways in which a philosopher may hypostatize a power. To think of an ability as a piece of property which may be passed from one owner to another, as in the fairy-tale, is one way. Another way, by contrast, is to think of an ability as the kind of thing one might have two of. (Roger Bannister had an ability to run a four-minute mile, as he proved by doing so. Does it make sense to ask how many such abilities he had – as opposed to asking whether he had the ability to do it more than once?) A third way is to treat the relationship between an ability and its exercise as a contingent and not a logical matter. The presence of an ability does not account for its exercise in the way that the presence of a vehicle does; you may explain how opium puts people to sleep by saying that it contains morphine, but not by saying that it has a *virtus dormitiva*. Hypostatizations of powers in this way are futile because any power, as Aquinas says, is defined by its exercise and individuated by its possessor (*S* 1–2,54,2; *S* 1,29,1).

Aquinas frequently warns against the dangers of hypostatizing in this way. He points out, for instance, that accidents (and most powers are accidents, in his system) are ultimately attributes of substances, not of other accidents (*S* 1,77,5c; 1–2,50,2). He insists that there cannot be more than one form of a given kind in a given subject (*S* 1–2,51,4).

Yet when he comes to treat of the soul and its powers, he seems to waver in the application of these principles. Thus, when he addresses the question how many powers there are in the soul, he observes that according to Aristotle there is a scale of being.

Things which are at the bottom of this scale achieve little by means of little movement; next above come things which achieve much but with much activity; highest of all are those things which achieve much with little or no activity. Aquinas continues:

> Thus the person in the worst state of health is the one who not only lacks perfect health, but also needs a few medicines to enjoy such health as he has; better off is the person who can enjoy perfect health, but only with a large number of medicines; better again is the person who needs few medicines, and best of all is the person who enjoys perfect health with no medicine at all.

The parallel is then drawn, to enable us to decide how many powers there are in the human soul:

> Sub-human creatures achieve particular goods, and do so by means of a limited number of determined activities and powers. Human beings can achieve a universal goodness, because they can obtain happiness; but they are at the bottom level of those beings capable of happiness, so that the human soul requires many and various activities and powers. For angels a smaller range of powers suffices, and in God there are no powers or activities other than his essence.
>
> $(S\ 1,77,2)^9$

It is difficult, in reading passages such as this, to know whether or not Aquinas is guilty of the error of hypostatizing abilities. On the one hand, the comparison between medicines and powers is a very dangerous one: it is just the kind of comparison that would be made by a philosopher who had failed to distinguish between abilities and their vehicles. On the other hand, when Aquinas is describing the hierarchy of possessors of powers, he speaks constantly of the multiplicity of powers *and activities*, as if to show that he is aware of the futility of multiplying powers without multiplying their exercises. Elsewhere, however, there are similar passages which seem to be less cautious. When Aquinas says, for instance, that the higher an angel is in the celestial hierarchy the more he can know with fewer dispositions (S 1–2,50,6), we wonder on what principle abilities can be counted except by reference to the number of individuals possessing them and the number of things which they are an ability to do. After more than thirty years of reading

Aquinas, I still find it difficult to decide whether his apparent hypostatization of powers is merely a matter of incautious expression, or is a sign of deep philosophical confusion. I must leave the question, as they say, as an exercise for the reader.

Notes

1 WHY READ AQUINAS?

1 Unpublished manuscript, MS 213, 424.

2 MIND AND METAPHYSICS

1 Videtur quod Deus non habeat liberum arbitrium.

1. Dicit enim Hieronymus, in homilia de Filio Prodigo: Solus Deus est, in quem peccatum non cadit, nec cadere potest; cetera, cum sint liberi arbitrii, in utramque partem flecti possunt.

2. Praeterea, liberum arbitrium est facultas rationis et voluntatis, qua bonum et malum eligitur. Sed Deus non vult malum, ut dictum est. Ergo liberum arbitrium non est in Deo.

Sed contra est quod dicit Ambrosius, in libro De Fide: Spiritus Sanctus dividit singulis prout vult, idest pro liberae voluntatis arbitrio, non necessitatis obsequio.

Respondeo dicendum quod liberum arbitrium habemus respectu eorum quae non necessario volumus, vel naturali instinctu. Non enim ad liberum arbitrium pertinet quod volumus esse felices, sed ad naturalem instinctum. Unde et alia animalia, quae naturali instinctu moventur ad aliquid, non dicuntur libero arbitrio moveri. Cum igitur Deus ex necessitate suam bonitatem velit, alia vero non ex necessitate, ut supra ostensum est; respectu illorum quae non ex necessitate vult, liberum arbitrium habet.

Ad primum ergo dicendum quod Hieronymus videtur excludere a Deo liberum arbitrium, non simpliciter, sed solum quantum ad hoc quod est deflecti in peccatum.

Ad secundum dicendum quod, cum malum culpae dicatur per aversionem a voluntate divina, per quam Deus omnia vult, ut supra ostensum est, manifestum est quod impossibile est eum malum culpae velle. Et tamen ad opposita se habet, inquantum velle potest hoc esse vel non esse. Sicut et nos, non peccando, possumus velle sedere, et non velle sedere.

3 PERCEPTION AND IMAGINATION

1 Naturali appetitu quaelibet potentia desiderat sibi conveniens. Sed appetitus animalis consequitur formam apprehensam. Et ad huiusmodi appetitum requiritur specialis animae potentia, et non sufficit sola apprehensio. Res enim appetitur prout est in sua natura. Non est autem secundum suam naturam in virtute apprehensiva, sed secundum suam similitudinem. Unde patet quod visus appetit naturaliter visibile solum ad suum actum, scilicet ad videndum, animal autem appetit rem visam per vim appetitivam, non solum ad videndum, sed etiam ad alios usus.

2 Est autem sensus quaedam potentia passiva, quae nata est immutari ab exteriori sensibili (*S* 1,78,3).

3 Est autem duplex immutatio, una naturalis et alia spiritualis: naturalis quidem, secundum quod forma immutantis recipitur in immutato secundum esse naturale, sicut calor in calefacto; spiritualis autem secundum quod forma immutantis recipitur in immutato secundum esse spirituale, ut forma coloris in pupilla, quae non fit per hoc colorata. Ad operationem autem sensus requiritur immutatio spiritualis per quam intentio formae sensibilis fiat in organo sensus. Alioquin, si sola immutatio naturalis sufficeret ad sentiendum, omnia corpora naturalia sentirent dum alterantur.

4 THE NATURE OF THE INTELLECT

1 In . . . creaturis intellectualibus intellectus est quaedam potentia intelligentis.

2 Because of the overtones of the Latin word *pati*, from which the notion of passive power is derived, Aquinas has to make rather heavy weather of the fact that the kind of change involved does not involve any actual *suffering* for the intellect.

3 Secundum opinionem Platonis, nulla necessitas erat ponere intellectum agentem ad faciendum intelligibilia in actu; sed forte ad praebendum lumen intelligibile intelligenti, ut infra dicetur. Posuit enim Plato formas rerum naturalium sine materia subsistere, et per consequens eas intelligibiles esse: quia ex hoc est aliquid intelligibile actu, quod est immateriale. Et huiusmodi vocabat species, sive ideas, ex quarum participatione dicebat etiam materiam corporalem formari, ad hoc quod individua naturaliter constituerentur in propriis generibus et speciebus; et intellectus nostros, ad hoc quod de generibus et speciebus rerum scientiam haberent.

Sed quia Aristoteles non posuit formas rerum naturalium subsistere sine materia; formae autem in materia existentes non sunt intelligibiles actu: sequebatur quod naturae seu formae rerum sensibilium, quas intelligimus, non essent intelligibiles actu. Nihil autem reducitur de potentia in actum, nisi per aliquod ens actu: sicut sensus fit in actu per sensibile in actu. Oportebat igitur ponere aliquam virtutem ex parte intellectus, quae faceret intelligibilia in actu, per abstractionem specierum a conditionibus materialibus. Et haec est necessitas ponendi intellectum agentem.

4 Plato, ut posset salvare certam cognitionem veritatis a nobis per intellectum haberi, posuit praeter ista corporalia aliud genus entium a materia et motu separatum, quod nominabat species sive ideas, per quarum participationem unumquodque istorum singularium et sensibilium dicitur vel homo vel equus vel aliquid huiusmodi. Sic ergo dicebat scientias et definitiones et quidquid ad actum intellectus pertinent, non referri ad ista corpora sensibilia, sed ad illa immaterialia et separata; ut sic anima non intelligat ista corporalia, sed intelligat horum corporalium species separatas.

5 Videtur autem in hoc Plato deviasse a veritate, quia, cum aestimaret omnem cognitionem per modum alicuius similitudinis esse, credidit quod forma cogniti ex necessitate sit in cognoscente eo modo quo est in cognito. Consideravit autem quod forma rei intellectae est in intellectu universaliter et immaterialiter et immobiliter: quod ex ipsa operatione intellectus apparet, qui intelligit universaliter et per modum necessitatis cuiusdam; modus enim actionis est secundum modum formae agentis. Et ideo existimavit quod oporteret res intellectas hoc modo in seipsis subsistere, scilicet immaterialiter et immobiliter. Hoc autem necessarium non est.

6 *Compositio et divisio* means literally: putting together and taking apart. An instance of a *compositio* would be the judgement 'arsenic is poisonous'; an instance of a *divisio* would be 'arsenic is not poisonous'. By 'putting together' Aquinas does not mean the putting together of the words 'arsenic' and 'poisonous'; this is something which occurs in both the positive and the negative sentences. He calls the positive sentence a putting together because it states that arsenic and poisonousness are as it were put together in reality, and the negative sentence a taking apart because it states that arsenic and poisonousness are as it were far apart from each other in reality. Aquinas explains this at *H* 1,3,26.

7 Intellectus enim nostri, secundum Philosophum in lib. de Anima, duplex est operatio. Una qua format simplices rerum quidditates; ut quid est homo, vel quid est animal: in qua quidem operatione non invenitur verum per se nec falsum, sicut nec in vocibus incomplexis. Alia operatio intellectus est secundum quam componit et dividit, affirmando et negando: et in hac iam invenitur verum et falsum, sicut et in voce complexa, quae est eius signum.

8 Verbum intellectus nostri, secundum cuius similitudinem loqui possumus de verbo in divinis, est id ad quod operatio intellectus nostri terminatur, quod est ipsum intellectum, quod dicitur conceptio intellectus; sive sit conceptio significabilis per vocem incomplexam, ut accidit quando intellectus format quidditates rerum; sive per vocem complexam, quod accidit quando intellectus componit et dividit.

9 Si intellectus agens compararetur ad intellectum possibilem ut obiectum agens ad potentiam, sicut visibile in actu ad visum, sequeretur quod statim omnia intelligeremus, cum intellectus agens sit quo est omnia facere. Nunc autem non se habet ut obiectum, sed ut faciens

obiecta in actu: ad quod requiritur, praeter praesentiam intellectus agentis, praesentia phantasmatum, et bona dispositio virum sensitivarum, et exercitium in huiusmodi opere; quia per unum intellectum fiunt etiam alia intellecta, sicut per terminos propositiones, et per prima principia conclusiones.

10 Dicit enim in III de Anima, quod, cum intellectus possibilis sic fiat singula ut sciens, dicitur qui secundum actum; et quod hoc accidit cum possit operari per seipsum. Est quidem igitur et tunc potentia quodammodo; non tamen similiter ut ante addiscere aut invenire. Dicitur autem intellectus possibilis fieri singula, secundum quod recipit species singulorum. Ex hoc ergo quod recepit species intelligibilium, habet quod potest operari cum voluerit, non autem quod semper operetur; quia et tunc est quodammodo in potentia, licet aliter quam ante intelligere; eo scilicet modo quo sciens in habitu est in potentia ad considerandum in actu.

11 Memoria praeteritorum est. Sed praeteritum dicitur secundum aliquod determinatum tempus. Memoria igitur est cognoscitiva alicuius sub determinato tempore; quod est cognoscere aliquid sub hic et nunc. Hoc autem non est intellectus sed sensus. Memoria igitur non est in parte intellectiva, sed solum in parte sensitiva.

12 Praeteritio potest ad duo referri: scilicet ad obiectum quod cognoscitur; et ad cognitionis actum. Quae quidem duo simul coniunguntur in parte sensitiva, quae est apprehensiva alicuius per hoc quod immutatur a praesenti sensibili: unde simul animal memoratur se prius sensisse in praeterito, et se sensisse quoddam praeteritum sensibile. Sed quantum ad partem intellectivam pertinet, praeteritio accidit, et non per se convenit, ex parte obiecti intellectus.

13 Intelligere animae nostrae est quidam particularis actus, in hoc vel in illo tempore existens, secundum quod dicitur homo intelligere nunc vel heri vel cras. Et hoc non repugnat intellectualitati . . . sicut intelligit seipsum intellectus, quamvis ipse sit quidam singularis intellectus, ita intelligit suum intelligere, quod est singularis actus vel in praeterito vel in praesenti vel in futuro existens.

14 Ratio et intellectus in homine non possunt esse diversae potentiae. Quod manifeste cognoscitur, si utriusque actus consideretur. Intelligere enim est simpliciter veritatem intelligibilem apprehendere. Ratiocinari autem est procedere de uno intellecto ad aliud, ad veritatem intelligibilem cognoscendam . . . . Patet ergo quod ratiocinari comparatur ad intelligere sicut moveri ad quiescere, vel acquirere ad habere.

15 See above, p. 49.

5 APPETITE AND WILL

1 Quamlibet formam sequitur aliqua inclinatio: sicut ignis ex sua forma inclinatur in superiorem locum, et ad hoc quod generet sibi simile . . . . In his enim quae cognitione carent, invenitur tantummodo forma ad unum esse proprium determinans unumquodque, quod etiam naturale uniuscuiusque est. Hanc igitur formam naturalem sequitur naturalis

inclinatio, quae appetitus naturalis vocatur. In habentibus autem cognitionem, sic determinatur unumquodque ad proprium esse naturale per formam naturalem, quod tamen est receptivum specierum aliarum rerum: sicut sensus recipit species omnium sensibilium, et intellectus omnium intelligibilium, ut sic anima hominis sit omnia quodammodo secundum sensum et intellectum.

2 Cognitio intellectiva est universalium, et secundum hoc distinguitur a sensitiva, quae est singularium. Sed ista distinctio non habet locum ex parte appetitivae: cum enim appetitus sit motus ab anima ad res, quae sunt singulares, omnis appetitus videtur esse rei singularis. Non ergo appetitus intellectivus debet distingui a sensitivo.

3 Unaquaeque potentia animae est quaedam forma seu natura, et habet naturalem inclinationem in aliquid. Unde unaquaeque appetit obiectum sibi conveniens naturali appetitu. Supra quem est appetitus animalis consequens apprehensionem, quo appetitur aliquid non ea ratione qua est conveniens ad actum huius vel illius potentiae, utpote visio ad videndum et auditio ad audiendum; sed quia est conveniens simpliciter animali.

4 The tradition which he tries to harmonize goes back ultimately to a familiar passage in Plato's *Republic* where we are introduced to a tripartite soul.

5 In aliis enim animalibus statim ad appetitum concupiscibilis et irascibilis sequitur motus, sicut ovis, timens lupum, statim fugit: quia non est in eis aliquis superior appetitus qui repugnet. Sed homo non statim movetur secundum appetitum irascibilis et concupiscibilis; sed expectatur imperium voluntatis, quod est appetitus superior.

6 Sic igitur anima dicitur dominari corpori despotico principatu: quia corporis membra in nullo resistere possunt imperio animae, sed statim ad appetitum animae moventur manus et pes, et quodlibet membrum quod natum est moveri voluntario motu. Intellectus autem, seu ratio, dicitur principari irascibili et concupiscibili politico principatu: quia appetitus sensibilis habet aliquod proprium, unde potest reniti imperio rationis. Natus est enim moveri appetitus sensitivus, non solum ab aestimativa in aliis animalibus, et cogitativa in homine, quam dirigit universalis ratio; sed etiam ab imaginativa et sensu. Unde experimur irascibilem vel concupiscibilem rationi repugnare, per hoc quod sentimus vel imaginamur aliquod delectabile quod ratio vetat, vel triste quod ratio praecipit. Et sic per hoc quod irascibilis et concupiscibilis in aliquo rationi repugnant, non excluditur quin ei obediant.

7 Necesse est enim quod non potest non esse. Quod quidem convenit alicui, uno modo ex principio extrinseco: sive materiali, sicut cum dicimus quod omne compositum ex contrariis necesse est corrumpi; sive formali, sicut cum dicimus quod necesse est triangulum habere tres angulos aequales duobus rectis. Et haec est necessitas naturalis et absoluta. Alio modo convenit alicui quod non possit non esse, ex aliquo intrinseco, vel fine vel agente. Fine quidem, sicut cum aliquis non potest sine hoc consequi, aut bene consequi, finem aliquem: ut cibus dicitur necessarius ad vitam, et equus ad iter. Et haec vocatur necessitas finis; quae interdum etiam utilitas dicitur. Ex agente autem

hoc alicui convenit, sicut cum aliquis cogitur ab aliquo agente, ita quod non possit contrarium agere. Et haec vocatur necessitas coactionis.

8 Sicut intellectus ex necessitate inhaeret primis principiis, ita voluntas ex necessitate inhaereat ultimo fini, qui est beatitudo: finis enim se habet in operativis sicut principium in speculativis, ut dicitur in II Physic.

9 Sunt autem quaedam intelligibilia quae non habent necessariam connexionem ad prima principia; sicut contingentes propositiones, ad quarum remotionem non sequitur remotio primorum principiorum. Et talibus non ex necessitate assentit intellectus. Quaedam autem propositiones sunt necessariae, quae habent connexionem necessariam cum primis principiis, sicut conclusiones demonstrabiles, ad quarum remotionem sequitur remotio primorum principionem. Et his intellectus ex necessitate assentit, cognita connexione necessaria conclusionum ad principia per demonstrationis deductionem: non autem ex necessitate assentit antequam huiusmodi necessitatem connexionis per demonstrationem cognoscat.

Similiter etiam est ex parte voluntatis. Sunt enim quaedam particularia bona, quae non habent necessariam connexionem ad beatitudinem, quia sine his potest aliquis esse beatus: et huiusmodi voluntas non de necessitate inhaeret. Sunt autem quaedam habentia necessariam connexionem ad beatitudinem, quibus scilicet homo Deo inhaeret, in quo solo vera beatitudo consistit. Sed tamen antequam per certitudinem divinae visionis necessitas huiusmodi connexionis demonstretur, voluntas non ex necessitate Deo inhaeret, nec his quae Dei sunt.

10 Actio intellectus consistit in hoc quod ratio rei intellectae est in intelligente; actus vero voluntatis perficitur in hoc quod voluntas inclinatur ad ipsam rem prout in se est. Et ideo Philosophus dicit, in VI Metaphys. quod bonum et malum quae sunt objecta voluntatis, sunt in rebus; verum et falsum, quae sunt objecta intellectus, sunt in mente. Quando igitur res in qua est bonum, est nobilior ipsa anima, in qua est ratio intellecta; per comparationem ad talem rem, voluntas est altior intellectu. Quando vero res in qua est bonum, est infra animam; tunc etiam per comparationem ad talem rem, intellectus est altior voluntate. Unde melior est amor Dei quam cognitio: e contrario autem melior est cognitio rerum corporalium quam amor.

11 Nihil velle possumus nisi sit intellectum. Si igitur ad intelligendum movet voluntas volendo intelligere, oportebit quod etiam illud velle praecedat aliud intelligere, et illud intelligere aliud velle, et sic in infinitum: quod est impossibile.

12 See Kenny, 1992, p.72.

6   THE FREEDOM OF THE WILL

1 Quaedam agunt absque iudicio: sicut lapis movetur deorsum; et similiter omnia cognitione carentia. Quaedam autem agunt iudicio, sed non libero; sicut animalia bruta. Iudicat enim ovis videns lupum, eum esse fugiendum, naturali iudicio, et non libero; quia non ex collatione, sed ex naturali instinctu hoc iudicat. Et simile est de quolibet iudicio brutorum animalium. Sed homo agit iudicio: quia per vim cognoscitivam iudicat

aliquid esse fugiendum vel prosequendum. Sed quia iudicium istud non est ex naturali instinctu in particulari operabili, sed ex collatione quadam rationis, ideo agit libero iudicio, potens in diversa ferri. Ratio enim circa contingentia habet viam ad opposita . . . . Particularia autem operabilia sunt quaedam contingentia: et ideo circa ea iudicium rationis ad diversa se habet, et non est determinatum ad unum. Et pro tanto necesse est quod homo sit liberi aribitrii, ex hoc ipso quod rationalis est.

2 Homo per liberum arbitrium seipsum movet ad agendum. Non tamen hoc est de necessitate libertatis, quod sit prima causa sui id quod liberum est; sicut nec ad hoc quod aliquid sit causa alterius, requiritur quod sit prima causa eius. Deus igitur est prima causa movens et naturales causas et voluntarias. Et sicut naturalibus causis, movendo eas, non aufert quin actus earum sint naturales; ita movendo causas voluntarias, non aufert quin actiones earum sint voluntariae, sed potius hoc in eis facit: operatur enim in unoquoque secundum eius proprietatem.

3 Ex parte vero corporis et virtutum corpori annexarum, potest esse homo aliqualis naturali qualitati, secundum quod est talis complexionis, vel talis dispositionis, ex quacumque impressione corporearum causarum: quae non possunt in intellectivam partem imprimere, eo quod non est aliquis corporis actus. Sic igitur qualis unusquisque est secundum corpoream qualitatem, talis finis videtur ei: quia ex huiusmodi dispositione homo inclinatur ad eligendum aliquid vel repudiandum. Sed istae inclinationes subiacent iudicio rationis, cui obedit inferior appetitus, ut dictum est. Unde per hoc libertati arbitrii non praeiudicatur.

4 Ad electionem autem concurrit aliquid ex parte cognitivae virtutis, et aliquid ex parte appetitivae; ex parte quidem cognitivae, requiritur consilium, per quod diiudicatur quid sit alteri praeferendum; ex parte autem appetitivae, requiritur quod appetendo acceptetur id quod per consilium diiudicatur . . . . Proprium obiectum electionis est illud quod est ad finem: hoc autem, inquantum huiusmodi, habet rationem boni quod dicitur utile; unde cum bonum, inquantum huiusmodi, sit obiectum appetitus, sequitur quod electio sit principaliter actus appetitivae virtutis. Et sic liberum arbitrium est appetitiva potentia.

5 Ex parte appetitus, velle importat simplicem appetitum alicuius rei: unde voluntas dicitur esse de fine, qui propter se appetitur. Eligere autem est appetere aliquid propter alterum consequendum: unde proprie est eorum quae sunt ad finem. Sicut autem se habet in cognitivis principium ad conclusionem, cui propter principia assentimus, ita in appetitivis se habet finis ad ea quae sunt ad finem, quae propter finem appetuntur. Unde manifestum est quod sicut se habet intellectus ad rationem, ita se habet voluntas ad vim electivam, idest ad liberum arbitrium. Ostensum est autem supra, quod eiusdem potentiae est intelligere et ratiocinari, sicut eiusdem virtutis est quiescere et moveri. Unde etiam eiusdem potentiae est velle et eligere. Et propter hoc voluntas et liberum arbitrium non sunt duae potentiae, sed una.

6 Ad rationem voluntarii requiritur quod principium actus sit intra, cum aliqua cognitione finis. Est autem duplex cognitio finis: perfecta scilicet, et imperfecta. Perfecta quidem finis cognitio est quando non

solum apprehenditur res quae est finis, sed etiam cognoscitur ratio finis, et proportio eius quod ordinatur in finem ad ipsum. Et talis cognitio finis competit soli rationali naturae. Imperfecta autem cognitio finis est quae in sola finis apprehensione consistit, sine hoc quod cognoscatur ratio finis, et proportio actus ad finem. Et talis cognitio finis invenitur in brutis animalibus, per sensum et aestimationem naturalem.

7 Iudicium autem est in potestate iudicantis secundum quod potest de suo iudicio iudicare: de eo enim quod est in nostra potestate, possumus iudicare. Iudicare autem de iudicio suo est solius rationis, quae super actum suum reflectitur, et cognoscit habitudines rerum de quibus iudicat, et per quas iudicat: unde totius libertatis radix est in ratione constituta.

8 Copleston, 1955, 194.

9 For example, Actus voluntatis nihil est aliud quam inclinatio quaedam procedens ab interiori principio cognoscente (1a 2ae,6,4).

10 All that is necessary for it to be true that there is an act of my will is that 'I want' (in the appropriate sense) is true of me. This is clear especially in *De Malo* 6c.

11 In a number of places I have tried to work out in detail the comparison between willing and commanding that lies behind Aquinas' theory of *actus imperatus*. The analogy has been dignified by the name 'The Imperative Theory of the Will'. It is discussed in Kenny, 1963, 203–39; Kenny, 1975, 27–45; Kenny, 1989, 40–4.

7 SENSE, IMAGINATION AND INTELLECT

1 Priores vero Naturales, quia considerabant res cognitas esse corporeas et materiales, posuerunt oportere res cognitas etiam in anima cognoscente materialiter esse. Et ideo, ut animae attribuerent omnium cognitionem, posuerunt eam habere naturam communem cum omnibus. Et quia natura principiatorum ex principiis constituitur, attribuerunt animae naturam principii: ita quod qui dixit principium omnium esse ignem, posuit animam esse de natura ignis; et similiter de aere et aqua.

2 Hoc non videtur convenienter dictum. Primo quidem quia, si habet anima naturalem notitiam omnium, non videtur esse possibile quod huius naturalis notitiae tantum oblivionem capiat, quod nesciat se huiusmodi scientiam habere: nullus enim homo obliviscitur ea quae naturaliter cognoscit, sicut quod omne totum sit maius sua parte, et alia huiusmodi. Praecipue autem hoc videtur inconveniens, si ponatur esse naturale corpori uniri, ut supra habitum est: inconveniens enim est quod naturalis operatio alicuius rei totaliter impediatur per id quod est sibi secundum naturam. Secundo, manifeste apparet huius positionis falsitas ex hoc quod, deficiente aliquo sensu, deficit scientia eorum quae apprehenduntur secundum illum sensum; sicut caecus natus nullam potest habere notitiam de coloribus. Quod non esset, si animae essent naturaliter inditae omnium intelligibilium rationes.

3 Intellectum vero posuit Aristoteles habere operationem absque communicatione corporis. Nihil autem corporeum imprimere potest in rem

incorpoream. Et ideo ad causandum intellectualem operationem, secundum Aristotelem, non sufficit sola impressio sensibilium corporum, sed requiritur aliquid nobilius . . . illud superius et nobilius agens quod vocat intellectum agentem, de quo iam supra diximus, facit phantasmata a sensibus accepta intelligibilia in actu, per modum abstractionis cuiusdam.

4 Forma sensibilis alio modo est in re quae est extra animam, et alio modo in sensu, qui suscipit formas sensibilium absque materia, sicut colorem auri sine auro. Et similiter intellectus species corporum, quae sunt materiales et mobiles, recipit immaterialiter et immobiliter, secundum modum suum.

5 Aristoteles autem media via processit. Posuit enim cum Platone intellectum differre a sensu. Sed sensum posuit propriam operationem non habere sine communicatione corporis; ita quod sentire non sit actus animae tantum, sed coniuncti . . . . In hoc Aristoteles cum Democrito concordavit, quod operationes sensitivae partis causentur per impressionem sensibilium in sensum . . . . Intellectum vero posuit Aristoteles habere operationem absque communicatione corporis. Nihil autem corporeum imprimere potest in rem incorpoream. Et ideo ad causandam intellectualem operationem, secundum Aristotelem, non sufficit sola impressio sensibilium corporum, sed aliquid nobilius.

6 Videtur quod intellectus possit actu intelligere per species intelligibiles quas penes se habet, non convertendo se ad phantasmata. Intellectus enim fit in actu per speciem intelligibilem qua informatur. Sed intellectum esse in actu, est ipsum intelligere. Ergo species intelligibiles sufficient ad hoc quod intellectus actu intelligat, absque hoc quod ad phantasmata se convertat.

7 De ratione naturae lapidis est, quod sit in hoc lapide; et de ratione naturae equi est, quod sit in hoc equo: et sic de aliis. Unde natura lapidis, vel cuiuscumque materialis rei cognosci non potest complete, et vere, nisi secundum quod cognoscitur ut in particulari existens: particulare autem apprehendimus per sensum et imaginationem. Et ideo, necesse est, ad hoc quod intellectus actu intelligat suum obiectum proprium, quod convertat se ad phantasmata, ut speculetur naturam universalem in particulari existentem.

8 Incorporalium non sunt aliqua phantasmata: quia imaginatio tempus et continuum non transcendit. Si ergo intellectus noster non potest aliquid intelligere in actu nisi converteretur ad phantasmata, sequeretur quod non posset intelligere incorporeum aliquid.

9 Incorporea, quorum non sunt phantasmata, cognoscuntur a nobis per comparationem ad corpora sensibilia, quorum sunt phantasmata . . . et ideo cum de huiusmodi aliquid intelligimus, necesse habemus converti ad phantasmata corporum, licet ipsorum non sint phantasmata.

8 UNIVERSALS OF THOUGHT

1 Secundum hoc ergo, ex parte phantasmatum intellectualis operatio a sensu causatur. Sed quia phantasmata non sufficiunt immutare intellectum possibilem, sed oportet quod fiant intelligibilia actu per intel-

lectum agentem; non potest dici quod sensibilis cognitio sit totalis et perfecta causa intellectualis cognitionis, sed magis quodammodo est materia causae.

2 Proprium [intellectus humani] est cognoscere formam in materia quidem corporali individualiter existentem, non tamen prout est in tali materia. Cognoscere vero id quod est in materia individuali, non prout est in tali materia, est abstrahere formam a materia individuali, quam repraesentant phantasmata.

3 Ea quae pertinent ad rationem speciei cuiuslibet rei materialis, puta lapidis aut hominis aut equi, possunt considerari sine principiis individualibus, quae non sunt de ratione speciei. Et hoc est abstrahere universale a particulari, vel speciem intelligibilem a phantasmatibus, considerare scilicet naturam speciei absque consideratione individualium principiorum, quae per phantasmata repraesentantur.

4 Virtute intellectus agentis resultat quaedam similitudo in intellectu possibili ex conversione intellectus agentis supra phantasmata quae quidem est repraesentativa eorum quae sunt phantasmata, solum quantum ad naturam speciei. Et per hunc modum dicitur abstrahi species intelligibilis a phantasmatibus: non quod aliqua eadem numero forma, quae prius fuit in phantasmatibus postmodum fiat in intellectu possibili.

5 Quicumque enim intellectus intelligit rem aliter quam sit est falsus. Formae autem rerum materialium non sunt abstractae a particularibus, quorum similitudines sunt phantasmata. Si ergo intelligamus res materiales per abstractionem specierum a phantasmatibus, erit falsitas in intellectu nostro.

6 Quidam posuerunt quod vires cognoscitivae quae sunt in nobis nihil cognoscunt nisi proprias passiones; puta quod sensus non sentit nisi passionem sui organi. Et secundum hoc, intellectus non intelligit nisi suam passionem, idest speciem intelligibilem in se receptam. Et secundum hoc, species huiusmodi est ipsum quod intelligitur.

Sed haec opinio manifeste apparet falsa . . . . Si igitur ea quae intelligimus essent solum species quae sunt in anima, sequeretur quod scientiae omnes non essent de rebus quae sunt extra animam, sed solum de speciebus intelligibilibus quae sunt in anima.

7 Sed quia intellectus supra seipsum reflectitur, secundum eandem reflexionem intelligit et suum intelligere et speciem qua intelligit. Et sic species intellectiva secundario est id quod intelligitur.

8 Similiter forma secundum quam provenit actio manens in agente est similitudo obiecti. Unde similitudo rei visibilis est secundum quam visus videt; et similitudo rei intellectae, quae est species intelligibilis, est forma secundum quam intellectus intelligit.

9 Cognitio intellectiva aliquo modo a sensitiva primordium sumit. Et quia sensus est singularium, intellectus autem universalium; necesse est quod cognitio singularium, quoad nos, prior sit quam universalium cognitio.

10 Puer a principio prius distinguit hominem a non homine, quam distinguat hunc hominem ab alio homine; et ideo pueri a principio appellant omnes viros patres, posterius autem determinant unumquemque, ut dicitur.

11 Si autem consideremus ipsam naturam generis et speciei prout est in

singularibus, sic quoddamodo habet rationem principii formalis respectu singularium: nam singulare est propter materiam, ratio vero speciei sumitur ex forma. Sed natura generis comparatur ad naturam speciei magis per modum materialis principii: quia natura generis sumitur ab eo quod est materiale in re, ratio vero speciei ab eo quod est formale; sicut ratio animalis a sensitivo, ratio vero hominis ab intellectivo.

9   KNOWLEDGE OF PARTICULARS

1 Si quis astrologus cognosceret omnes motus caeli et distantias caelestium corporum, cognosceret unamquamque eclipsim quae futura est usque ad centum annos; non tamen cognosceret eam inquantum est singulare quoddam, ut sciret eam nunc esse vel non esse, sicut rusticus cognoscit dum eam videt. Et hoc modo ponunt Deum singularia cognoscere; non quasi singularem naturam eorum inspiciat, sed per positionem causarum universalium. Ex causis universalibus non consequuntur nisi formae universales, si non sit aliquid per quod formae individuentur. Ex formis autem universalibus congregatis, quotcumque fuerint, non constituitur aliquid singulare; quia adhuc collectio illarum formarum potest intelligi in pluribus esse.

2 Dicendum quod singulare in rebus materialibus intellectus noster directe et primo cognoscere non potest. Cuius ratio est, quia principium singularitatis in rebus materialibus est materia individualis: intellectus autem noster, sicut supra dictum est, intelligit abstrahendo speciem intelligibilem ab huiusmodi materia. Quod autem a materia individuali abstrahitur est universale. Unde intellectus noster directe non est cognoscitivus nisi universalium.

3 Indirecte autem, et quasi per quandam reflexionem, potest cognoscere singulare: quia, sicut supra dictum est, etiam postquam species intelligibiles abstraxit, non potest secundum eas actu intelligere nisi convertendo se ad phantasmata, in quibus species intelligibiles intelligit, ut dicitur. Sic igitur ipsum universale per speciem intelligibilem directe intelligit; indirecte autem singularia, quorum sunt phantasmata. Et hoc modo format hanc propositionem, Socrates est homo.

4 In rebus autem materialibus non invenitur infinitum in actu, sed solum in potentia, secundum quod unum succedit alteri. Et ideo in intellectu nostro invenitur infinitum in potentia, in accipiendo unum post aliud: quia nunquam intellectus noster tot intelligit, quin possit plura intelligere.

5 Dicendum quod contingentia dupliciter possunt considerari. Uno modo, secundum quod contingentia sunt. Alio modo, secundum quod in eis aliquid necessitatis invenitur: nihil enim est adeo contingens quin in se aliquid necessarium habeat. Sicut hoc ipsum quod est Socratem currere in se quidem contingens est; sed habitudo cursus ad motum est necessaria: necessarium enim est Socratem moveri, si currit.

Est autem unumquodque contingens ex parte materiae: quia contingens est quod potest esse et non esse: potentia autem pertinet ad materiam. Necessitas autem consequitur rationem formae: quia ea quae consequuntur ad formam ex necessitate insunt. Materia autem est individuationis principium: ratio autem universalis accipitur secundum abstractionem formae a materia particulari. Dictum autem est supra quod per se et directe intellectus est universalium; sensus autem singularium, quorum etiam indirecte quodammodo est intellectus, ut supra dictum est.

Sic igitur contingentia, prout sunt contingentia, cognoscuntur directe quidem sensu, indirecte autem ab intellectu: rationes autem universales et necessariae contingentium cognoscuntur per intellectum.

Unde si attendantur rationes universales scibilium, omnes scientiae sunt de necessariis. Si autem attendantur ipsae res, sic quaedam scientia est de necessariis, quaedam vero de contingentibus.

10 SELF-KNOWLEDGE

1 Consequens est ut sic seipsum intelligat intellectus noster, secundum quod fit actu per species a sensibilibus abstractas per lumen intellectus agentis . . . . Non ergo per essentiam suam, sed per actum suum se cognoscit intellectus noster.

2 Ad primam cognitionem de mente habendam, sufficit ipsa mentis praesentia, quae est principium actus ex quo mens percipit seipsam.

3 Id quod primo cognoscitur ab intellectu humano est huiusmodi obiectum; et secundario cognoscitur ipse actus quo cognoscitur obiectum; et per actum cognoscitur ipse intellectus, cuius est perfectio ipsum intelligere.

4 Talis autem est praedicta copulatio intellectus possibilis ad hominem, in quo sunt phantasmata quorum species sunt in intellectu possibili, qualis est copulatio parietis in quo est color, ad visum in quo est species sui coloris. Sicut igitur paries non videt, sed videtur eius color; ita sequeretur quod homo non intelligeret, sed quod eius phantasmata intelligerentur ab intellectu possibili.

11 THE NATURE OF THE SOUL

1 Necesse est dicere id quod est principium intellectualis operationis, quod dicimus animam hominis, esse quoddam principium incorporeum et subsistens. Manifestum est enim quod homo per intellectum cognoscere potest naturas omnium corporum. Quod autem potest cognoscere aliqua oportet ut nihil eorum habeat in sua natura, quia illud quod inesset ei naturaliter impediret cognitionem aliorum, sicut videmus quod lingua infirmi quae infecta est cholerico et amaro humore non potest percipere aliquid dulce, sed omnia videntur ei amara. Si igitur principium intellectuale haberet in se naturam alicuius corporis, non posset omnia corpora cognoscere. Omne autem corpus habet aliquam naturam determinatam. Impossibile est igitur quod principium intellectuale sit corpus.

2 Ipsum igitur intellectuale principium quod dicitur mens vel intellectus habet operationem per se cui non communicat corpus. Nihil autem

potest per se operari nisi quod per se subsistit; non enim est operari nisi entis in actu, unde eo modo aliquid operatur quo est. Propter quod non dicimus quod calor calefacit, sed calidum. Relinquitur igitur animam humanam, quae dicitur intellectus vel mens, esse aliquid incorporeum et subsistens.

3 Omne quod est subsistens potest dici operari. Sed anima non dicitur operari; quia, ut dicitur in *De Anima*, dicere animam sentire aut intelligere simile est ac si dicat eam aliquid texere vel aedificare. Ergo anima non est aliquid subsistens.

4 Operationes partium attribuuntur toti per partes. Dicimus enim quod homo videt per oculum et palpat per manum aliter quam calidum calefacit per calorem, quia calor nullo modo calefacit proprie loquendo. Potest igitur dici quod anima intelligit sicut oculus videt, sed magis proprie dicitur quod homo intelligat per animam.

5 The sense in which this is true has been discussed above, p. 95.

6 See p. 138.

7 Cum igitur sentire sit quaedam operatio hominis, licet non propria, manifestum est quod homo non est anima tantum, sed est aliquid compositum ex anima et corpore.

8 Quidam posuerunt solam formam esse de ratione speciei, materiam vero esse partem individui et non speciei. Quod quidem non potest esse verum. Nam ad naturam speciei pertinet id quod significat definitio. Definitio in rebus naturalibus non significat formam tantum, sed formam et materiam, unde materia est pars speciei in rebus naturalibus; non quidem materia signata, quae est principium individuationis, sed materia communis. Sicut enim de ratione huius hominis est quod sit ex hac anima et his carnibus et his ossibus, ita de ratione hominis est quod sit ex anima et carnibus et ossibus.

9 Constat quod homo naturaliter desiderat salutem sui ipsius, anima autem cum sit pars corporis hominis, non est totus homo, et anima mea non est ego; unde licet anima consequatur salutem in alia vita, non tamen ego vel quilibet homo. In I ad Corinthios XV, 1,11 ed Cai, 924.

10 Sic autem cognoscitur unumquodque sicut forma eius est in cognoscente. Anima autem intellectiva cognoscit rem aliquam in sua natura absolute, puta lapidem inquantum est lapis absolute. Est igitur forma lapidis absolute, secundum propriam rationem formalem, in anima intellectiva. Anima igitur intellectiva est forma absoluta, non aliquid compositum ex materia et forma. Si enim anima intellectiva esset composita ex materia et forma, formae rerum reciperentur in ea ut individuales; et sic non cognosceret nisi singulare, sicut accidit in potentiis sensitivis, quae recipiunt formas rerum in organo corporali. Materia enim est principium individuationis formarum.

11 Solus Deus, qui est ipsum suum esse, est actus purus et infinitus. In substantiis intellectualibus est compositio ex actu et potentia, non quidem ex materia et forma, sed ex forma et esse participato. Unde a quibusdam dicuntur componi ex quo est et quod est.

12 Aquinas does offer a brief and unconvincing subsidiary argument to the following effect. The intellect can know truths which hold for all time. But desire follows knowledge. Therefore the intellect natur-

ally desires to exist for all time. But a natural desire cannot be futile. Therefore the intellect cannot pass away (*S* 1,75,6c).

13 In the final article of question seventy-five Aquinas inquires whether the soul is the same in kind as an angel. Sentimental Christian piety sometimes entertains the fancy that the souls of the dead – perhaps particularly of dead children – have become angels. Aquinas argues, on the contrary, that not only are human souls different in kind from angels, but that each angel is different in kind from another. Raphael and Gabriel, however similar they may be to each other, are not two individuals of the same species, because they have no matter to individuate them in the way in which matter individuates two animals of the same species.

12   MIND AND BODY

1 Dicendum quod necesse est dicere quod intellectus, qui est intellectualis operationis principium, sit humani corporis forma. Illud enim quo primo aliquid operatur est forma eius cui operatio attribuitur, sicut quo primo sanatur corpus est sanitas, et quo primo scit anima est scientia – unde sanitas est forma corporis et scientia animae. Et huius ratio est, quia nihil agit nisi secundum quod est actu; unde quo aliquid est actu, eo agit.

2 Manifestum est autem quod primum quo corpus vivit est anima. Et cum vita manifestetur secundum diversas operationes in diversis gradibus viventium id quo primo operamur unumquodque operum vitae est anima; anima enim est primum quo nutrimur et sentimus et movemur secundum locum, et similiter quo primum intelligimus. Hoc ergo principium quo primo intelligimus, sive dicatur intellectus sive anima intellectiva, est forma corporis.

3 Id quod per se habet esse non unitur corpori ut forma, quia forma est quo aliquid est, et sic ipsum esse formae non est ipsius formae secundum se. Sed intellectivum principium habet secundum se esse et est subsistens, ut supra dictum est. Non ergo unitur corpori ut forma.

4 Anima illud esse in quo ipsa subsistit communicat materiae corporali; ex qua et anima intellectiva fit unum ita quod illud esse quod est totius compositi est etiam ipsius animae. Quod non accidit in aliis formis quae non sunt subsistentes.

5 Quanto forma est nobilior, tanto magis dominatur materiae corporali et minus ei immergitur et magis sua operatione vel virtute excedit eam. Unde videmus quod forma mixti corporis habet aliquam operationem quae non causatur ex qualitatibus elementaribus. Et quanto magis proceditur in nobilitate formarum, tanto magis invenitur virtus formae materiam elementarem excedere, sicut anima vegetabilis plus quam forma metalli, et anima sensibilis plus quam anima vegetabilis. Anima autem humana est ultima in nobilitate formarum. Unde in tantum sua virtute excedit materiam corporalem quod habet aliquam operationem et virtutem in qua nullo modo communicat materia corporalis; et haec virtus dicitur intellectus.

6 Posset autem diversificari actio intellectualis mea et tua per diversit

atem phantasmatum, quia scilicet aliud est phantasma lapidis in me et aliud in te, si ipsum phantasma, secundum quod est aliud in me et aliud in te, esset forma intellectus possibilis. Quia idem agens secundum diversas formas rerum respectu eiusdem oculi sunt diversae visiones. Sed ipsum phantasma non est forma intellectus possibilis, sed species intelligibilis quae a phantasmatibus abstrahitur. In uno autem intellectu a phantasmatibus diversis eiusdem speciei non abstrahitur nisi una species intelligibilis . . . . Si ergo unus intellectus esset omnium hominum, diversitas phantasmatum quae sunt in hoc et in illo non posset causare diversitatem intellectualis operationis huius et illius hominis.

7 Dicendum est quod nulla alia forma substantialis est in homine nisi sola anima intellectiva, et quod ipsa, sicut virtute continet animam sensitivam et nutritivam, ita virtute continet omnes inferiores formas et facit ipsa sola quidquid imperfectiores formae in aliis faciunt.

8 Substantialis autem forma non solum est perfectio totius, sed cuiuslibet partis. Cum enim totum consistat ex partibus, forma totius quae non dat esse singulis partibus corporis est forma quae est compositio et ordo, sicut forma domus, et talis forma est accidentalis. Anima vero est forma substantialis, unde oportet quod sit forma et actus non solum totius, sed cuiuslibet partis. Et ideo recedente anima, sicut non dicitur animal et homo nisi aequivoce, quemadmodum et animal pictum vel lapideum, ita est de manu et oculo aut carne et osse, ut Philosophus dicit. Cuius signum est, quod nulla pars corporis habet proprium opus, anima recedente.

9 In rebus infima non possunt consequi perfectam bonitatem, sed aliquam imperfectam consequuntur paucis motibus: superiora his adipiscuntur perfectam bonitatem motibus paucis; summa vero perfectio invenitur in his quae absque motu perfectam possident bonitatem. Sicut infime est ad sanitatem dispositus qui non potest perfectam consequi sanitatem sed aliquam modicam consequitur paucis remediis; melius autem dispositus est qui potest perfectam consequi sanitatem, sed remediis multis; et adhuc melius, qui remediis paucis; optime autem qui absque remedio perfectam sanitatem habet. Dicendum est ergo quod res quae sunt infra hominem quaedam particularia bona consequuntur, et ideo quasdam paucas et determinatas operationes habent et virtutes. Homo autem potest consequi universalem bonitatem, quia potest adipisci beatitudinem; est tamen in ultimo gradu secundum naturam eorum quibus competit beatitudo, et ideo multis et diversis operationibus et virtutibus indiget anima humana. Angelis vero minor diversitas potentiarum competit. In Deo vero non est aliqua potentia vel actio praeter eius essentiam.

Further reading

A General introductory works

Anscombe, G. E. M. and Geach, P. T. *Three Philosophers*, Oxford, 1961.
Chenu, M. D. *Toward Understanding Saint Thomas*, trs A. M. Landry and D. Hughes, Chicago, 1964.
Copleston, F. C. *Aquinas*, London, 1955.
Davies, B. *The Thought of Thomas Aquinas*, Oxford, 1992.
Kenny, A. *Aquinas*, Oxford, 1980.
Kretzmann, N., Kenny, A. and Pinborg, J. *The Cambridge History of Later Medieval Philosophy*, Cambridge, 1982.
Marenbon, J. *Later Medieval Philosophy (1150–1350: An Introduction)*, London, 1987.
Weisheipl, J. *Friar Thomas d'Aquino: His Life, Thought and Works*, Oxford, 1974.

B Editions of the most relevant works of Aquinas

The Leonine edition (1882–), which will include all Aquinas' works, is incomplete and inconvenient to use. The edition of the commentary on the *De Anima*, by R. Gauthier, is the most useful of the volumes for Aquinas' philosophy of mind. More convenient, and commonly derived from the Leonine text, are the Marietti editions of particular works, including:

De Unitate Intellectus Contra Averroistas, ed. L. W. Keeler, Rome, 1936 (translation: *The Unicity of the Intellect*, R. Brennan, St Louis, 1946).
In Aristotelis Librum de Anima Commentarium, ed. A. M. Pirotta, Rome, 1959 (translation: *Aristotle's De Anima with the Commentary of St Thomas*, K. Foster and S. Humphries, London and New Haven, 1951).
In Libros Peri Hermeneias, ed. R. M. Spiazzi, Turin, 1955 (translation: *Aristotle on Interpretation – Commentary by St Thomas and Cajetan*, J. Oesterle, Milwaukee, 1962).
In X Libros Ethicorum, ed. R. M. Spiazzi, Turin, 1955 (translation: *Commentary on the Nicomachean Ethics*, C. J. Litzinger, Chicago, 1964).

Quaestiones Disputatae de Anima, ed. R. M. Spiazzi, Turin, 1947 (translation: *The Soul*, J. P. Rowan, St Louis, 1949).
Quaestiones Disputatae de Malo, ed. R. M. Spiazzi, Turin, 1949.
Quaestiones Disputatae de Veritate, ed. R. M. Spiazzi, Turin, 1953 (translation: *Truth*, R. W. Mulligan *et al.*, Chicago, 1952–4).
Summa Contra Gentiles, Rome, 1984 (translation: *On the Truth of the Catholic Faith*, A. C. Pegis *et al.*, Notre Dame, 1975).

For English readers, the best edition of the *Summa Theologiae* is the Blackfriars edition, London and New York, 1964–80, in sixty-one volumes, of which those most relevant to this book are:
Volume 11, *Man* (1a 75–83), ed. T. Suttor, 1970;
Volume 12, *Human Intelligence* (1a 84–9) ed. P. T. Durbin, 1968.

By far the best single-volume abbreviation of the *Summa* is Timothy McDermott's *Summa Theologiae: A Concise Translation*, London, 1989. Both the translation and the abridgement are excellent.

C Works relevant to Aquinas' philosophy of mind

Anscombe, G. E. M. *Intention*, Oxford, 1957.
Hoenen, P. *Reality and Judgment According to St Thomas*, trs H. F. Tiblier, Chicago, 1952.
Kenny, A. *Action, Emotion and Will*, London, 1963.
—— 'Intellect and Imagination in Aquinas', in Kenny, A. (ed.), *Aquinas: A Collection of Critical Essays*, Notre Dame, 1969.
—— *Will, Freedom and Power*, London, 1975.
—— 'Intentionality: Aquinas and Wittgenstein', in Kenny, A., *The Legacy of Wittgenstein*, Oxford, 1984.
—— *The Metaphysics of Mind*, Oxford, 1989.
—— *Aristotle on the Perfect Life*, Oxford, 1992.
Lonergan, B. *Verbum: Word and Idea in Aquinas*, Notre Dame, 1967.
Mahoney, E. 'Sense, Intellect and Imagination in Albert, Thomas and Siger', in Kretzmann, N., Kenny, A. and Pinborg, J., *The Cambridge History of Later Medieval Philosophy*, Cambridge, 1982.
McCabe, H. 'The Immortality of the Soul', in Kenny, A. (ed.), *Aquinas: A Collection of Critical Essays*, Notre Dame, 1969.
Peghaire, J. *'Intellectus' et 'ratio' selon S. Thomas d'Aquin*, Paris and Ottawa, 1936.

Index